Fixing Drugs

D1312934

Also by Sue Pryce

PRESIDENTIALIZING THE PREMIERSHIP: The Prime Ministerial Advisory System and the Constitution

Fixing Drugs

The Politics of Drug Prohibition

Sue Pryce

Associate Professor, School of Politics and International Relations,
University of Nottingham, UK

First published 2012 by
PALGRAVE MACMILLAN

Palgrave Macmillan in the UK is an imprint of Macmillan Publishers Limited, registered in England, company number 785998, of Houndmills, Basingstoke, Hampshire RG21 6XS.

Palgrave Macmillan in the US is a division of St Martin's Press LLC, 175 Fifth Avenue, New York, NY 10010.

Palgrave Macmillan is the global academic imprint of the above companies and has companies and representatives throughout the world.

Palgrave® and Macmillan® are registered trademarks in the United States, the United Kingdom, Europe and other countries.

ISBN 978–0-230–35970–3   hardback
ISBN 978–0-230–35971–0   paperback

This book is printed on paper suitable for recycling and made from fully managed and sustained forest sources. Logging, pulping and manufacturing processes are expected to conform to the environmental regulations of the country of origin.

A catalogue record for this book is available from the British Library.

A catalog record for this book is available from the Library of Congress.

10   9   8   7   6   5   4   3   2   1
21   20   19   18   17   16   15   14   13   12

Printed and bound in Great Britain by
CPI Antony Rowe, Chippenham and Eastbourne

*To Daniel for the knowledge
and
Robert for understanding*

'What experience and history teaches us is that people and governments have never learned anything from history, or acted on principles deduced from it.'

Hegel

Contents

Preface

One hundred years ago international drug prohibition began. On 23 January 1912 Germany, Italy, the Netherlands, Russia, China, the USA, Britain, Portugal, France, Siam (Thailand) and Persia (Iran) met in The Hague and signed the International Opium Convention, an agreement to ban all non-medical production, trade and use of drugs. Henceforth fixing drugs, or the problems they caused, was to be a matter of prohibition.

But there is no way of fixing drugs. The drug problem is unsolvable. Even the word 'problem' is problematical because it implies that there is a solution, whereas drug use is endemic, a part of the human condition. People want to use drugs, but drugs cause problems and that encourages those in authority to try to stop or strictly regulate drug use. There are many related problems that stem from both the use and prohibition of drugs. Some of these can be tackled, but often solutions create yet more problems, and the best all governments can hope to do is to mitigate some of the damaging effects of drug use.

Drugs are a major headache for states, particularly for those claiming to be both liberal and democratic. It is part of the democratic process that politicians seek our votes by promising to solve our problems. Few politicians would be willing to admit that drugs present a problem to be managed, not solved, by juggling a range of least-worst options. Some people believe drugs are wicked and should be prohibited. Drugs corrupt people and undermine society. Others believe that drugs are a nuisance because they cause more immediate problems. Drugs make people unfit for work, unfit for parenting and unworthy of citizenship. Pressure is exerted on the political authorities to take action. Politicians promise to get tough on drugs, enforce prohibition and deliver a drug-free world. But prohibition leads to a huge black market in illegal drugs. The immense profits this yields attract criminal gangs, the systemic violence of turf wars and 'contract' enforcement, a general disregard for the law, corruption of state institutions and damage to health and happiness. So authorities, in attempting to solve at least some of the problems associated with drugs, create many others and their efforts have little measurable effect on drug production or use themselves.

Someone who read the manuscript for this book described it as a polemic in favour of drug legalization. This surprised me. My only initial position for my work on drugs was curiosity. Why are some drugs banned but not others? As the mother of a heroin addict, I have experienced at first hand the heartache and financially devastating impact that drug use can have on near ones and dear ones, and had not set out to make a case for legalization. I was driven into a more polemical position when I saw that the arguments for world drug prohibition are so threadbare. Legalization might solve some aspect of the drug problem, but it is likely that it would result in an increase in drug use and therefore also of addiction, both of which harm individuals, families and societies. For those who wish to examine recent arguments in support of the continuation of pro-hibition, I recommend Professor Neil McKeganey's excellent work *Controversies in Drugs Policy and Practice* (2011), also published by Palgrave Macmillan.

Despite its title, this book does not set out to offer solutions to the drug problem. It accepts that it is unsolvable. It does not claim to be a comprehensive account of all aspects of the drug problem or of all the policies that have been tried to solve it. One volume could not do justice to a field of study beginning in Sumerian texts of 3000 BC which refer to the poppy as the 'plant of joy', to the contempo-rary international enforcement of prohibition. The question 'How would you explain this or that problem to an intelligent alien?' is a frequently used device when trying to encourage students to clarify their own understanding of a subject. This device is used here. This book seeks to provide explanations for what are some of the more baffling aspects of drug prohibition. It does so by posing and answer-ing a series of questions: how can the drug problem be explained? How can the difference between drugs that are regulated and those that are prohibited be explained? Why do states prohibit drugs? How do they try to enforce prohibition? What have been the conse-quences of this policy? Why does the international drug prohibition regime persist in the face of its own failure? Are we now witnessing the break-up of this already old drug regime as countries count the cost of its failure and begin to seek new ways of living with drugs?

Acknowledgements

I would like to thank Jim Young of DrugScope's Daily News for providing all those interested in this field with such an excellent news service. I would also like to thank all the students who have studied my Politics and Drugs and Narcoterrorism modules. They have helped to keep me on my toes and to maintain my enthusiasm. Thanks are also due to Amber Stone-Galilee, the Politics commissioning editor at Palgrave Macmillan, and her assistant Liz Blackmore, for all of their help and support in transforming this work for publication and to Nick Brock for his meticulous copy-editing. Finally, thanks to Ken for making and delivering all those cups of tea.

List of Abbreviations

ACMD	Advisory Council on the Misuse of Drugs
ATS	Amphetamine-type Stimulant
AUC	United Self-Defence Forces of Colombia (Autodefensas Unidas de Colombia)
CIA	Central Intelligence Agency (US)
CND	Commission on Narcotic Drugs (UN)
DEA	Drug Enforcement Administration (US)
ELN	National Liberation Army (Ejercito de Liberacion Nacional – Colombia)
EMCDDA	European Monitoring Centre for Drugs and Drug Addiction
FARC	Revolutionary Armed Forces of Colombia (Fuerzas Armadas Revolutionarias de Colombia)
FBI	Federal Bureau of Investigation (US)
IDPC	International Drug Policy Consortium
INCB	International Narcotics Control Board (UN)
NTA	National Treatment Agency (Britain)
TNI	Transnational Institute
UKDPC	United Kingdom Drug Policy Commission
UNDCP	United Nations Drug Control Programme
UNGASS	United Nations General Assembly Special Session (on drugs)
UNODC	United Nations Office on Drugs and Crime
WHO	World Health Organization
WOLA	Washington Office of Latin America

Glossary

Acquisitive crime This is also referred to as economic compulsive crime. It is used as a convenient shorthand to cover the types of crimes committed by problem drug users who cannot afford to pay for their drugs.

Addiction There is no authoritative definition. Some medical and neurological scientists argue that addiction does not exist. However, in relation to drugs it is commonly understood to refer to a cluster of characteristics including craving for a substance which eclipses other priorities, the development of tolerance so that a bigger dose is needed to gain the same effect, and unpleasant withdrawal symptoms.

Alternative development Alternative development is the name given to a comprehensive range of policies to encourage those who cultivate drug crops to switch production. It usually entails subsidies, crop substitution, training, improvements in infrastructure, improvements in the communications and transportation, irrigation (if needed), and refrigeration for perishable produce.

Amphetamine-type stimulants (ATSs) Commonly used shorthand for a range of synthetic stimulants, including amphetamines, methamphetamines, dextramphetamine (dexedrine) and ecstasy.

Balloon effect This is used to describe the way in which drug production and trafficking responds to enforcement in one area by moving to another. Eradication spraying in one coca-growing area leads to cultivation springing up elsewhere – further into the rainforest, for example. Relative success in interdicting cocaine across the Caribbean route via Florida into the USA resulted in an increase in trafficking via Mexico to the USA.

Certification The US Congress passed Drug Abuse Acts in 1986 and 1988 which required the president to make annual recommendations to Congress on whether or not countries that produce and traffic drugs are fighting their corner in the drug war, or at the very least cooperating with the USA on drug enforcement. If the president recommends that a country should be 'decertified' it is no longer eligible to receive US aid and the USA votes against it in international money-lending institutions. De-certification may also include trade sanctions. Countries that have been decertified at one time or another include Colombia, Nigeria, Myanmar and Bolivia.

Commission on Narcotic Drugs (CND) This was created in 1946 to be the UN policy-making body for drug-related matters.

Consumer countries These countries are 'net' importers of drugs. The producer/consumer country distinction has become blurred in recent years as traditional producer countries now often consume refined versions of their products and consumer countries are also producers of drugs such as ecstasy, LSD, amphetamines and cannabis.

Crop eradication This describes the destruction of illegal drug crops in the field, either manually or by use of chemical sprays.

Decriminalization This is a halfway house in which an activity remains unlawful but is no longer treated as a criminal offence. Lawbreakers do not get a criminal record. In some countries they may receive a fine or referral to a special panel which tries to persuade them to give up drug use.

Depenalization In this case an activity, drug use, remains a criminal offence but it no longer attracts a custodial sentence.

Designer drugs These drugs are deliberately created to evade the drug prohibition laws. Drugs that come into this category include what are referred to as 'legal highs'. Methedrone is an example of a designer drug which was launched as a legal high but is now prohibited in many countries.

Detox This is the commonly used abbreviation for detoxification. It involves the elimination of drugs from a user's body. It can be achieved either with or without medical aid to make withdrawal symptoms more tolerable.

Drug control regime A regime is a set of governing arrangements that affect relationships of interdependence in the international arena. The international drug control regime is a set of rules relating to the cultivation, production, trade and use of prohibited drugs worldwide. Signatories to the three UN anti-drugs conventions agree to incorporate these rules into their national law.

Drugs 'free-for-all' Often used by prohibitionists in a pejorative way to describe drug legalization. It implies that those arguing that drugs should be legalized want there to be no restrictions on access to drugs, whereas most advocates for legalization accept that it would be accompanied by some form of regulation stipulating the quantities and qualities of drugs and the age and access to drugs along the lines of alcohol and tobacco.

Drug rehabilitation This is more commonly referred to as 'rehab'. It refers to a medical and/or behavioural treatment for drug dependency. It involves not only detoxing the body from drugs, but also a process in which users develop an understanding of their former drug use and learn skills to resist drugs in the future and to live a drug-free and productive life.

Harm reduction/harm minimization This refers to a range of policies and practices which are intended to reduce the adverse health, social and economic consequences of the use of prohibited drugs, to users, their families and communities at large.

Interdiction This is a strategy that attempts to stop the drugs reaching the consumer. It is often used to refer to all those policies that try to interrupt the supply line from the crops in the field or chemicals in the laboratory, to prevent them reaching the street. It is based on the principle that if less drugs reach the street the price of those that do will rise and this will result in a fall in demand.

International Narcotics Control Board of the United Nations (INCB) The INCB was established by the 1961 Single Convention on Narcotic Drugs. It administers the system of annual estimates in which governments submit their needs for medical drugs that are controlled substances and it monitors the illicit drug trade and the adherence to the UN anti-drug conventions.

Medicalization This is a policy of regarding problems arising from drug use as a matter for treatment and health policy rather than punishment and enforcement. In Britain this was the outcome of recommendations of the Rolleston Report 1926.

Methadone This is an opioid, an opiate substitute commonly used to treat heroin addicts. By substituting a prescribed alternative to street drugs it is hoped that addicts will be able to live less chaotic lives and commit less acquisitive crime.

Militarization When this term is applied to anti-drug policy police and enforcement agencies, it involves using military-type weapons, strategies and rules of engagement. It also includes the use of armed forces in anti-drug operations. Mexico provides a contemporary example of militarized anti-drug initiative.

Narcotic Originally, this term was used to refer to opiates, sleep-inducing drugs, but is now widely used as a synonym for 'illegal drugs'.

Opiates Opiates are drugs extracted from opium poppies or derived from them. They include opium, morphine, codeine and heroin. Methadone is a synthetic opiate.

Opioids This refers to opiates as above, but also to synthetic drugs such as methadone and buprenorphine, which are commonly prescribed substitutes for opiates.

Psychopharmacological crime This term is used to describe the effect drugs have on a user's behaviour. It assumes that the chemical effect of a drug means users are more likely to commit crime, particularly violent crime.

Problem drug user In 1982 the ACMD introduced this concept. It defined a problem drug user as 'a person who experiences social, psychological, physical or legal problems related to intoxication and/or regular excessive consumption and/or dependence as a consequence of his own use of drugs'.

Precursor chemicals These chemicals play an essential role in the processing of organic plant material into drugs. Acetic anhydride is used in the production of heroin; sodium carbonate, kerosene, hydrochloric acid and potassium permanganate are used in the production of cocaine. Chemicals are also the basis of synthetic drugs. The 1988 UN Convention against Illicit Traffic in Narcotic Drugs and Psychotropic Substances incorporates the illicit trade in these chemicals into the drug control regime. However, these chemicals are widely used in the production of everyday goods and industrial processes and this makes it difficult to monitor their diversion to illicit uses. Since 2006 the Commission on Narcotic Drugs requires governments to provide annual estimates of their national licit requirements for these chemicals in order to prevent 'leakage' to the illicit market.

Producer countries Those countries that have traditionally been associated with the production of the plant-based drugs, cocaine, heroin, cannabis. Today most producer countries are also consumer countries. Not only do their citizens grow drug crops and consume them in traditional ways, such as chewing coca leaves in the Andean countries, but they also now use refined versions of the drug, cocaine and crack. Contemporary use of the term 'producer countries' refers to those countries that are net exporters of drugs, for example Afghanistan, Colombia.

Psychoactive drug This is a drug that affects the mood, feelings and perceptions of the user.

Recreational drugs Usually describes drugs that are used for pleasure and from which drug users appear to suffer no problems.

Systemic crime This describes those crimes that arise because drugs are traded in an illegal market in which violence and intimidation are used to enforce contracts and settle turf wars.

Tolerance When used in the drug world this refers to the way a body adapts to drug use and requires increased doses to maintain the same effect.

Transactional crime This is a type of crime which involves illegal trade between willing participants.

United Nations Commission on Narcotic Drugs (CND) This is the main policy-making agency for drug control. It is composed of 30 members of the UN Economic and Social Council and makes recommendations about drugs policy to the Council.

United Nations 1961 Single Convention on Narcotic Drugs This simplified and consolidated under the UN previous drug control machinery and treaties that had evolved since the 1912 Hague Convention.

United Nations 1971 Convention on Psychotropic Substances This extended controls to drugs not covered by the 1961 Single Convention. In particular, it included synthetic drugs including amphetamines, tranquilizers and LSD into the prohibition regime.

United Nations 1988 Convention against the Illicit Traffic in Narcotic Drugs and Psychotropic Substances Signatories to this Convention agree to monitor the financial institutions and commercial records in order to identify and prosecute money-laundering activities. They also agree to cooperate with each other in all aspects of drug control, and it extends controls and monitoring to the trade in precursor chemicals.

United Nations Office on Drugs and Crime (UNODC) This was established in 1997 as the Office of Drug Control and Crime Prevention, but gained its current name in 2002. It coordinates responses to drug trafficking and drug misuse and includes within its remit crime prevention, international terrorism and corruption.

War on drugs In 1971 President Richard Nixon declared war on drugs. The term is used in a more general sense to describe the efforts of governments to enforce their anti-drug laws, which in most cases are a reflection of the three UN anti-drug conventions. The drug war includes both domestic and foreign policy strategies and it encourages the idea that drugs are like an invading army that crosses borders and an internal enemy of the state that threatens security.

Timeline

1971	United Nations Convention on Psychotropic Substances ratified
	Misuse of Drugs Act passed in Britain
	Richard Nixon declares war on drugs
1973	Drug Enforcement Administration created in the USA
1976	The Netherlands introduces a tolerant approach to cannabis
1982	Ronald Reagan securitizes drug problem
1985	Nancy Reagan launches 'Just Say No' campaign
1986	US Congress passed Anti-Drug Abuse Amendment Act requiring presidents to certify that countries receiving US aid are pursuing anti-drug policies
1988	United Nations Convention against Illicit Traffic in Narcotic Drugs and Psychotropic Substances agreed
1990	Switzerland reviews its drug policy and introduces heroin prescriptions for addicts
1993	Pablo Escobar killed
1995	USA decertifies Colombia
1998	United Nations AIDS conference urges an increase in needle exchange programmes worldwide to halt the spread of AIDS virus through illicit drug injections
	United Nations General Assembly launches decade against drug abuse
	United Nations Drug Control Programme established
2000	Plan Colombia agreed between the USA and Colombia – supported by the EU
2001	Portugal decriminalizes possession of drugs
2005	Evo Morales launches 'Coca Yes Cocaine No' campaign
2006	President Calderón reinvigorates the drug war in Mexico
2008	Merida Initiative – US Congress agreed $400 million anti-drugs aid package for Mexico and Central American states

2010   Proposition 19, to legalize cannabis, defeated in California by 56 votes to 44

2011   Report of the Global Commission on Drug Policy calls for rethink of prohibition

1
Introduction

If people did not like using drugs, and authorities did not fear their effects, there would be no drug problem. The prohibition of one drug or another has long been a policy issue for different countries, but we now have experience of a hundred years of failed international drug control and, since the 1970s, the outright prohibition of an ambitiously long and growing list of drugs. In an age of evidence-based policy, when the evidence points overwhelmingly to abject failure, it is hard to explain why 185 out of approximately 200 countries in the world still support the international drug prohibition regime which has as its ultimate aim of freeing the world of all drugs. Despite this regime, the illegal drugs trade is thriving, with an estimated annual value of between $300 billion and $500 billion (UN World Drug Report, 2005), and ranks in the top three global industries alongside arms and oil. All indices of policy measurement show that prohibition has failed. The authorities seize larger and larger consignments of drugs, yet there are more drugs and more types of drugs available everywhere; they are often stronger and cheaper than in the 1960s; they are increasingly used by a younger age group and growing numbers of drug users are coming forward for treatment for addiction.

It is of course important to bear in mind that figures are not facts when it comes to drugs. It is not easy to produce reliable statistics about an illegal trade. Much reliance has to be placed on self-reporting both within individual countries and thence to the United Nations Office of Drugs and Crime (UNODC). Those who provide the figures often have a reason either to exaggerate or to minimize the numbers they use. The police and the drug agencies often 'big up' the scale of their drug seizures to show their effectiveness. McAllister, for instance, tells us, 'In the US, the chief purveyor of addiction statistics through the latter years of the 1960s, the Federal Bureau of Narcotics, adjusted the numbers of addicts reported, sometimes abruptly, to suit its own purpose' (McAllister, 2000, 5). Users often exaggerate the amount they use to get more generous substitute prescriptions to re-sell or make up for reduced access to their real drug of choice. Besides, users known to the authorities represent only a tiny minority of drug users worldwide. Despite this lack of robust data, common sense tells us that, far from a drug-free world, drug use has increased unabated throughout the last hundred years of control and prohibition. Norm Stamper, the former chief of police of Seattle, makes the point more forcefully: 'we've spent a trillion dollars prosecuting the war on drugs. What do we have to show for it? Drugs are more readily available, at lower prices and higher levels of potency. It's a dismal failure' (cit. Engel, 2009).

Drugs do cause problems, and, if we accept the arguments of those who would like to see the legalization of all drugs, many of these problems are caused by drug prohibition rather than by the drugs themselves. Prohibition has provided incentives for a complex and sophisticated network of international drug gangs, widespread violence, the corruption of state institutions, the involuntary displacement of people and environmental damage. Prohibition has led to a range of health problems among drug users caused by drugs of doubtful purity and unpredictable strength, dirty user equipment and ignorance about safe using practices. The trade in prohibited drugs has also provided the finance for insurgents and international terrorists.

So the question has to be asked: why, in the face of all this evidence, do states still try to prohibit drugs? Why do they persist in the face of consistent policy failure? Belief systems offer one important explanation. If drugs are wicked and corrupt the individual and the state, then it will always be worth fighting to stop people using them.

Drug use can be traced to earliest times, but so too can feelings of unease about drugs and their effects and disapproval of those who use them. Human beings have a long and complex relationship with drugs. We seem driven to find and use, eat, drink, inhale, chew or inject substances which have stimulant, sedative, euphoriant or hallucinatory effects (Weil, 1986, 3). Research also reveals that it is not only humans that are attracted to drugs. A variety of animal species from starlings to reindeer also make use of drugs (Haynes, 2010).

Many owners of domestic cats will be familiar with the effects of catnip on the behaviour of their pets. But animals do not share our ambivalence to drugs. We are attracted to these substances, but at the same time we fear them. Escape from a mean, humdrum, miserable life has always been a human desire. Human beings, particularly the young, try drugs, because, like the mountain, they are there. They offer risk, excitement, novelty and pleasure. The modern world, with its globalized economy and globalizing culture, means that the drug mountain is always there for everybody. Almost all types of drugs are available almost everywhere, at a price. Human beings need security but they also crave risk and this is provided by drugs. People try drugs for a variety of reasons: curiosity, peer pressure, the expectation of pleasure, enhanced perception, and the desire to escape. The risks provided by drugs are actually increased by prohibition since illegal drugs carry increased risks associated with the unknown purity of the product and also the risk of punishment. They offer an opportunity for young people to rebel against parents, society and the law. The contemporary high-tech world has raised expectations for instant gratification and drugs provide it. Life is seen through a TV or computer screen, so why not see life through the chemical screen of drugs?

There is, of course, a downside. One of the most feared outcomes of drug use is addiction. Addiction is a contested concept (see Dalrymple, 2007, and Royal College of Psychiatrists and Royal College of Physicians 2000, henceforth RCPsy and RC Phys) but for the drug user and the person in the street, the meaning of addiction is quite clear. It is an invisible line which divides the casual, recreational user from the compulsive user. The addict craves a particular drug, develops a tolerance that gives rise to the need for larger and larger doses to gain the same effect, experiences unpleasant withdrawal symptoms if drug use is brought to a halt, and often neglects other interests, pleasures and responsibilities. The addict ceases to control his drug use and instead becomes controlled by his drug. The most fundamental advocates of prohibition believe that all drug users will eventually become addicts.

These beliefs about drugs and their potentially destructive effects give rise to the cry that something must be done! If users cannot control their drug use, then the authorities must take steps to do so. Attempts to solve the drug problem mean that the authorities must regulate access to drugs or even prohibit access altogether, for the individual's own good and the good of all.

This fundamentalist way of thinking informs the international drug prohibition regime, a set of rules that have been agreed for governing our relationship with drugs. This rests on a belief that the world can be saved from the ravages of drugs through the implementation of a series of international agreements banning the cultivation, manufacture and distribution of drugs. This ideological explanation for drug prohibition is reinforced by a variety of explanations arising from economics, social policy and politics, and has produced a massive prohibition industry to equal the enemy, the drugs industry. Ideology helps to explain the persistence of drug prohibition, but why is it that only *some* drugs are outlawed? Are some drugs more wicked or dangerous than others? Certainly those people brought up in the war against drugs have been encouraged to believe that not all drugs are equally wicked.

The next chapter will explore the answer to the question of which drugs states regard as problematical. Which drugs are perceived to be more threatening than others? Chapter 3 will examine why states fear drugs, consider the source of our beliefs about drugs, and what economic, social and political factors reinforce these beliefs? States' fear and hatred of drugs has been translated into a policy of prohibition. This entails not only declaring drugs to be illegal; it also calls for a series of policies intended to bring about a drug-free world. An examination of these measures will be the subject of chapter 4. It has been noted already that prohibition may cause more problems than it solves. Chapter 5 will examine the unintended consequences of prohibition that make the persistence of prohibition even more difficult to explain. Chapter 6 will offer some explanations for the persistence of prohibition. Often, at the very moment when the value or usefulness of something is questioned and defended most vehemently, it signals that it has in fact already ceased to operate. Chapter 7 asks whether this is what is now happening to drug prohibition. Is the international drug prohibition regime already breaking up? The rhetoric of the drug war remains tough, but the will to create a drug-free world is quietly disappearing. Now the reality of policy may not even be containment: stopping the spread of drug use. International drug policy is still predicated on the wickedness of drugs and the principle of the greatest happiness of the greatest number, but in reality it has become a modest rearguard action to limit the extent of social harm. In the context of these de facto changes, chapter 8 will explore the alternatives now being suggested for fixing drugs.

2
Which Drugs Are Problems for States?

All drugs are a problem, but some drugs are more problematical than others. Therefore, although states dislike and fear drugs they do not dislike and fear all drugs equally. The drugs they dislike change over time and different states dislike and fear different drugs. Why is it, if we are over 18 (in Britain), we can buy and drink as much cheap, strong cider as we want from supermarkets, but if we are caught in possession of a small quantity of cannabis, we face an escalating scale of penalties that can end in a prison sentence of up to five years? To answer this we must first decide what is a drug?

The word 'drug' is a generic term used to describe prescribed medicines, over-the-counter remedies and psychoactive substances. Historically most states have welcomed most medicines although they have frequently regulated access to them. In Britain, for example, drugs that come under the heading of antibiotics, such as penicillin or erythromycin, can usually only be obtained from a pharmacist on the authority of a doctor's prescription. But even medicines can present problems. Some may be too costly for state medical services; interferon, for example, is a very costly treatment for AIDS that is beyond the budget of many developing countries. Some medicines may have shocking side effects, as was the case, for example, with thalidomide in the 1960s, a drug which was prescribed to combat morning sickness in pregnancy but which in many cases resulted in foetal malformations. The governments of modern states tend to get the blame for these kinds of shortcomings. States' apparatus encompass agencies, such as the US Food and Drug Agency and the British Medicines and Health Agency, which investigate claims made for the medicines before they are cleared for public consumption. Some medicines are widely accessible, allowing people to treat their own minor aches and pains without resort to a doctor. Many of these 'cures' are on sale in supermarkets, although for some cures there are formalities to be observed, such as a pharmacist being on hand to provide advice and warn of the dangers of usage. But we do not usually associate the 'drug problem' with either prescribed medicines or over-the-counter remedies, although there are some concerns about the abuse of prescribed tranquillizers and pain killers. Robin McKie's article, 'US Stars Are Falling Victim to Prescription Drugs' with the subheading 'Thousands of Britons are also addicted to painkillers and other pills obtained legally from GPs or on the internet', explores this increasingly troubling aspect of drug misuse (McKie, 2009).

It is some of the drugs that fall under the heading of psychoactive substances that are the focus of fear and source of controversy. Psychoactive substances affect mood, thought processes and perception and these include legal substances which are unregulated and available over the counter, like coffee, regulated but available substances, such as alcohol and tobacco, and substances which are currently illegal like cocaine, heroin, cannabis, the plant-based substances, and a variety of synthetics including ecstasy, amphetamines and LSD (RCPsy and RCPhys 2000, 261). It is this latter group of prohibited substances that are the subject of this book.

Despite the ubiquitous American 'drug store', the contemporary use of the term 'drug' is politically and morally loaded. We tend to reserve the term 'drug' for prohibited psychoactive substances. Vincenzo Ruggiero notes that 'drug is not a descriptive but an evaluative concept' (Ruggiero, 1999, 123), that is, it implies prohibition. What distinguishes a 'drug' is its legal status and the moral and social disapproval it arouses. This helps to explain why it is that, despite their psychoactive and addictive properties, tobacco and alcohol are rarely described as drugs in America and Europe, although this is beginning to change. In the UK, for example, the term 'drug' is usually reserved for those substances prohibited under the 1971 Misuse of Drugs Act, which categorizes drugs in classes and sections according to their perceived danger and uses. Those in class A are regarded as the most dangerous. The list of prohibitions is flexible. Substances can be classified, declassified and reclassified. The act established the Advisory Council on the Misuse of Drugs (ACMD), to make recommendations to the British government on the danger of drugs and how they should be classified. In 2004, on the advice of the ACMD, the government lowered cannabis from class B to class C. Cannabis was placed in class C in recognition that it was less dangerous than other class B drugs and because its popularity made it a very expensive drug to police. It was restored to class B on the grounds that the most commonly used cannabis is 'skunk', a much stronger type of the drug than those types used in the past. This latter change was made by the government despite the ACMD's recommendation that cannabis should remain in class C.

So it is governments who decide what a drug is, but on what do they base their decisions? How do governments make this divide between legal and illegal substances? Do they base it on scientific medical knowledge, that drugs are dangerous so the public must be protected from them? There is very little evidence for this argument. Simon Jenkins, bemoaning the fact that the British government was about to reclassify cannabis back up to class B, described it as: 'This obscure decision, taken in defiance of the Advisory Council on the Misuse of Drugs, is a vignette of modern British government. Brown [PM Gordon Brown] has no evidence to alter what is a pharmacological classification, but is happy to abuse science to "send a message".' He goes on to say that the message is not intended for cannabis users, who would in any case ignore it, but for 'the editor of the *Daily Mail*' (Jenkins, 2010; see also *Observer* editorial, 1 November 2009 'Drugs: Prejudice and Political Weakness Have Rejected Scientific Facts'). Pharmacologically. there is no difference between those psychoactive substances that are legal and those that are not. Many claim, in fact, that those psychoactive substances that are legal are equally, if not more dangerous and addictive, and that their impact on societies is just as damaging as those which are illegal (Trebach and Inciardi, 1993, 24; Weil, 1986, 41). Professor David Nutt, the chair of the ACMD at the time cannabis was reclassified to class B, was subsequently removed from his position for making just such a claim. Philip Johnston argues that 'Professor Nutt's offence was to say that cannabis causes less harm than alcohol and tobacco, not just to the health of the individual consumer but also in a wider sense, especially the violence associated with binge drinking' (Johnston, 2009).

The apparent randomness of the process by which a psychoactive substance becomes classified as a 'drug' can be illustrated by a case study of the treatment of two drugs: tobacco and coca.

A tale of two drugs

	Tobacco	Coca
What is it?	Naturally occurring plant: nicotiana	Naturally occurring plant: Erythroxylum
How is it used?	Chewed Smoked – pipes; cigars; cigarettes Snorted – snuff	Chewed Derivatives: **Cocaine** hydrochloride – snorted; injected **Crack** – smoked in pipe; injected
Why use it?	Stimulant Aids concentration Suppresses appetite Pleasure	Stimulant Fight altitude sickness Fight fatigue Powerful local anaesthetic still used in ear, nose and throat surgery -formerly used in dentistry
Problems	Tolerance Addiction Health – bronchial diseases; lung, throat and mouth cancers heart disease, strokes	Tolerance Addiction Possible sudden high blood pressure/heart attack Nose damage Paranoia, psychosis
Social problems	Impact on non-smokers; less socially acceptable in the West than in the past	Illegal therefore high cost of black market product Knock-on effect on citizenship, users and suppliers ignoring law Acquisitive crime to pay for high cost of drug High costs of policing and criminal justice Criminal records
Estimated global usage	1.25 billion people smoke cigarettes	14.3 million

The table gives a snapshot of the surprising similarities between these two substances. It should be noted that tobacco is regarded as one product, even though it is used in several ways, but in the case of coca, outside the Andes region, it is primarily the processed forms of coca, cocaine and crack cocaine, that are most widely used.

People have a variety of reasons for trying tobacco: positive advertising; positive image association; peer pressure; expectation of pleasure. New users may experience nausea but very quickly tobacco becomes addictive and users develop a tolerance for the substance, encouraging the user to smoke more to gain the same degree of satisfaction. Smoking devices have been found on archaeological sites in South America dating back 3,000 years, but it was only introduced into Europe in the sixteenth century (Wilbert, 1987, xvii). It was smoked by rolling the leaves and setting light to them, something along the lines of an early cigar. Nicotine, the active ingredient of tobacco, is a stimulant that acts on the pleasure centres of the brain (Edwards, 2004, 19). Smokers claim that a cigarette makes them feel calmer and more relaxed, but it is just as likely that what smokers claim to be the soothing properties of the drug are in fact simply relief from intermittent withdrawal symptoms (ibid., 20). Tobacco smoking is blamed for a wide range of bronchial ailments, heart problems and cancer. In Britain cigarette smoking is blamed for 80,000 deaths every year (Department of Health, 2009). Certainly it is widely accepted that nicotine is a highly addictive substance and some studies have regarded it as being as addictive as heroin (RCPsy and RCPhys, 2000, 19). If nicotine is administered intravenously its effects are almost indistinguishable from those of cocaine (ibid.).

Cocaine is a derivative of the coca plant, erythroxylum. For many centuries the leaves of this plant have been used as a stimulant by the peoples of the Andes region. The leaves, along with an alkaline additive, are formed into a wad in the side of the mouth and sucked slowly to release their stimulant properties and to maintain a low but constant level of cocaine in their bloodstream (Edwards, 2004, 20). This suppresses the appetite, increases energy and helps to combat the effects of altitude sickness. Coca has undergone two major transformations. In the nineteenth century cocaine hydrochloride was extracted, commonly referred to simply as cocaine. It was found that the stimulant effect could be intensified by snorting the powder up the nostrils or by use of intravenous injection. In the 1980s cocaine itself was further refined (by a process of adding water and bicarbonate of soda) to form crack, which is usually smoked in a pipe, although it can also be used intravenously. Crack delivers a faster and more intense high than cocaine, but this is followed by an equally intense come down. Cocaine is reputedly more addictive than coca, and crack more addictive than cocaine. Cocaine and crack can lead to sudden high blood pressure and heart attacks. Prolonged heavy use can lead to paranoia and psychosis (see Honer et al., 1987; Manschreck et al., 1988). The frequent snorting of cocaine powder can result in damage to the nasal passages. The figures for deaths caused by cocaine and crack in England and Wales are considerably lower than for those attributed to tobacco. In 2009 there were 202 deaths that were classified as involving cocaine use (Office of National Statistics, 2010). However, such figures must be treated with caution. Cocaine use is a covert activity, the number of users can only be estimated and causes of death are often difficult to attribute to use of a single substance (ibid.).

Tobacco and coca have some strikingly similar characteristics: both are stimulants, both are addictive and both can have adverse effects on the health of the user. Coca and its derivatives do have some medical uses, whereas tobacco has none. However, their different legal status means that tobacco is a highly taxed legal product that contributes considerable revenue to the treasuries of both producer and consumer countries. Coca and its derivatives are prohibited and regarded as enemies in the international drug war. The countries that grow, process and trade in coca are regarded as pariah states, subjected to international disapprobation and intervention in their internal affairs.

At the start of this chapter it was noted that the definition of a drug changes over time. Today, heroin, a member of the opiate family of drugs sourced from the opium poppy, is regarded as a great demon drug, if not *the* demon drug. Denis Zorin, a priest and former addict, describes heroin as 'the world's evil . . . it is comparable to a chemical weapon, capable of destroying our society quietly without much noise' (cit. Nemtsova, 2010). John Kaplan's book about the heroin problem, *Heroin: the Hardest Drug* (Kaplan, 1983), clearly reinforces this view. Drug users, even those who are beginning to use heroin, consider heroin to be a kind of crossing of the Rubicon of drug use. There can be little doubt that heroin has wrecked the lives of many users as well as those of their familes and friends. But heroin has not always had a bad name, nor does it always have one today. In 1874, when C.R. Alder Wright at St Mary's

Hospital London first discovered heroin as a derivative of opium, it was hailed as a wonder drug. Addiction in general had been known about for centuries, but at this time there was little understanding of the addictive properties of heroin. Opium was thought to be a cure for alcoholism; morphine, also an opiate, which was discovered in 1805 and was ten times stronger than opium, was hailed as a cure for opium addiction, and then heroin, which had an even greater euphoriant effect than morphine, was considered to offer a cure for morphine addiction. Opiate-based products, including those containing heroin, were readily available from corner shops. Laudanum, a distilled tincture of opium, received the ultimate seal of approval because Queen Victoria was reputed to be a regular user. Heroin was once viewed a popular 'cure all' used for pain relief and recreation. How then did heroin achieve its current status as public enemy number one? This can be explained in part by the growing awareness of the addictive properties of opiates which arose as a result of anti-drug pressure group activity at the turn of the century. The unrestricted prescribing of heroin-based medicines and the over-the-counter availability of patent medicines containing heroin caused awareness of a drug abuse problem on both sides of the Atlantic. Awareness of this danger signal was reinforced by American missionaries to China, who came home with horror stories about the destructive effects of opium addiction. These tales were given further credibility when, in 1898 following the Spanish–American war, America acquired the Philippines as a colony, and with it many opium addicts in its population. These factors coincided with the growing support for the temperance movement on both sides of the Atlantic and with the professional jealousy of pharmacists, which prompted them to seek a monopoly over the dispensing of medicines. By 1909 America had persuaded 13 key trading countries to attend the Shanghai Opium Convention. This heralded the beginning of the end of opiates as legal recreational drugs. However, in Britain, morphine kits complete with syringe and spare needles, labelled 'A Useful Gift for Friends at the Front', were still on sale in Harrods during the First World War (Robins, 2009, 165).

In a period of approximately 30 years, heroin, along with other opiates, moved from 'cure all' to the cause of all, or many, of society's problems and its use was prohibited in many countries. But opiates, and heroin in particular, are highly effective pain killers and, in

Britain, many people who undergo major surgery or who manage painful cancers and the like, are prescribed heroin, albeit heroin masked by its medical name of diamorphine. This is not to claim that heroin is not a 'dangerous' drug, but its reputation for causing death or serious health damage to individuals arises more from its illegal status than from any inherent chemical property. Recreational, and addicted, users who inject street heroin are dicing with death because they have no way of knowing the strength or purity of the drug they are injecting. This is something to which we will return when we explore the consequences of prohibition.

Throughout history there have been changes in the list of psychoactive substances that come to be feared and banned as drugs. Opium and heroin provide just two examples. But different states also have hostility towards different drugs. Internationally, the legal/illegal divide seems have been equally arbitrary. In the seventeenth century in Russia and in parts of Germany tobacco smoking was a capital offence. In Britain, although tobacco smoking was not prohibited, King James I issued his *Counterblaste to Tobacco* in 1604, in which he tried to discourage the use of tobacco by associating it with the 'barbarous and beastly manners of the wilde, godless and slavish Indians' (James I 1604). For centuries Europeans have tolerated the consumption of alcohol, whereas it is prohibited in Muslim countries. Mexican Indians legally use mescaline from the peyote cactus; Peruvian Indians chew coca to fight altitude sickness and hunger; cannabis and opium have always been used widely in the Indian subcontinent (RCPsy and RCPhys, 2000, 26–31, for a fuller account of drugs and culture see Coomber and South, 2004; Goodman et al., 2007; Klein, 2008).

If a 'drug' is defined neither by its active chemical composition nor by the damage it causes to health, then how is it defined? The distinction between legal and illegal substances derives from custom, convention and prejudice, reinforced by political ideology. Trebach summarizes the position: 'Over thousands of years of human history one drug or another has been banned or approved . . . not on the basis of science but due to the fears, prejudices, religious doctrines and political factors unique to a given culture and a particular historical era. Social or legal approval or disapproval is usually unrelated to the actual organic harm caused by drugs' (Trebach and Inciardi, 1993, 24).

But what is it about particular substances that arouse disapprobation at any one time and place? This can be explained in part by otherness and xenophobia. 'New' drugs (for example, tobacco in the seventeenth century), imports whose properties are not well understood and whose use is associated with immigrants (Murji, 1999, 49–65; Musto, 1999, 244–50) arouse fear of the unknown in native populations. They are often seen as foreign threats. In the 1920s, for example, the Alabama Congressman Richmond Hobson claimed that America had an immense number of heroin addicts and associated crime waves because of the evil influence of other nations. He described America as being 'surrounded by other dangerous continents. South America sent in cocaine, Europe contributed drugs like heroin and morphine, Asia was a source of crude opium and smoking opium; Africa produced hashish' (cit. Musto, 1999, 248). These sentiments were echoed 60 years later by the then UK Prime Minister Margaret Thatcher when she claimed, 'Britain – like the rest of Europe – is up against a determined effort to flood the country with hard drugs to corrupt our youth – to undermine the stability of our country' (*News of the World*, 20 October 1985). Collison offers a description of the way in which drugs and drug economies are viewed as 'other': 'Local communities in the industrial world are corrupted by outsiders – Mafiosi; Yardies; Colombians; Triads, or less poetically, existing criminal organisations' (Collison, 1996, 439; see also Ruggiero and South, 1997).

So a 'drug' can also be seen less as a medical or scientific term and more as an enemy to be identified and, in all its guises, feared, fought and defeated to safeguard a nation's citizens and way of life. Governments say which wicked substances are illegal and enforce the ban by imprisoning drug offenders like enemies of the state.

If 'drugs' are defined in part by their 'otherness', and there are different 'others' in different contemporary societies, why is it that in the twentieth century the same menu of drugs has come to be globally identified as the enemy in a universal crusade to create a drug-free world?

Until the twentieth century, drug problems were regarded as an issue for the attention of individual states. In the eighteenth century, Britain, for instance, considered itself to be in the grip of a gin craze, famously depicted in Hogarth's cartoons of 'Gin Lane'. It responded initially by prohibiting gin, but when this proved impossible, it opted for regulation (Dillon, 2002). In the nineteenth century, China responded to its widespread opium addiction problems by fighting, and losing, two Opium Wars (1839–42; 1856–60) against

Britain in an attempt to stop the British East India Company import-
ing opium into China. But it was the Shanghai Opium Commission
in 1909, followed by the 1912 Hague Convention on Opium, both
convened at the instigation of the USA, which signalled the internationalization of the drug problem. This has been followed by an
expanding body of international rules and regulations which seek
to control the use, production and trade of a lengthening list of
prohibited drugs. There are, in addition, controls over the sale of precursor chemicals used in drug manufacture, and controls over financial
transactions to detect and prosecute attempts to launder the profits
arising from the drug trade.

The result of this gradual expansion of drug control, sponsored by
America, under the auspices of the League of Nations and now the
United Nations, and urged on by Western European countries, is that
opium and its derivatives, cocaine and crack, cannabis and a range
of amphetamine-type stimulants (ATSs), are now either banned com-
pletely or limited to strictly medical or scientific purposes. The Royal
College of Psychiatrists and Royal College of Physicians Working
Party notes that

> International trade in alcoholic beverages and tobacco ... remains
> legal and unrestricted ... [while] trade in 'narcotics' is condemned
> as trafficking and subject to formidable penalties. International
> trade in alcohol and tobacco is actively encouraged and cannot be
> hindered without contravening the General Agreement on Tariffs
> and Trade. (RCPsy and RCPhys, 2000, 33)

This menu of illegal drugs reflects to a large extent the assumptions,
prejudices, customs and economic interests of the United States
and Western Europe which dominated the League of Nations in the
1920s and 1930s and the United Nations after 1945. America, the
UK and France had a huge investment in tobacco and alcohol. Their
cultural and economic hegemony enabled them to 'export their attitudes, customs and chosen drugs to the rest of the world' (RCPsy and
RCPhys, 2000, 33). If China, India and the Muslim world had been
the dominant powers, the menu of 'drugs' may have looked very
different. The belief that drugs are wicked is powerfully reinforced
by economic interest. All drugs may be wicked, but some drugs are
much more wicked than others.

All recreational drugs have always been problematical for those in authority. People have always experimented with chemically induced states of mind. Desire for intoxication, for the amelioration of existence, excitement, and the search for substances that will provide it, has been recorded since earliest antiquity. However, intoxication often transforms human behaviour in an anti-social way and so attracts the attention of authority. Authority, both sacred and secular, has tried to find ways to proscribe or severely limit access to these attractive but dangerous substances. Authority has tried to mediate this problem by regulating and permitting the use of some drugs but prohibiting others. Prohibition prevents people from using some drugs and punishes them if they do, or, if not the users, then the cultivators, manufacturers and dealers are pursued by the law. The dominant powers in the world have succeeded in persuading the rest to outlaw the menu of forbidden substances that they themselves have already banned. Prohibition has become the international fix for what is referred to as the 'drug problem'. If people did not enjoy using mind-altering substances prohibition would be unnecessary. The purpose of international prohibition is a world free from a particular, loaded, list of psychoactive substances that we generally call 'drugs'.

Having identified why people want to use psychoactive substances and how a particular list of psychoactive substances have come to be called 'drugs' and have been internationally outlawed, it is now time to look more closely at why states want to prohibit drug use. There is no doubt that drugs are high on the political agendas of many states. To explain the reason for this is we need to turn to ideological, economic, social and political explanations.

3
Why is There a Drug Problem at All?

There is a drug problem because people want to use drugs and states do not want them to. This leads to the question, why? States do not want people to use drugs because they fear the outcome: the possible collapse of the state. In this context the term state is used as shorthand to refer to those in authority who control the machinery of the state. It accepts that within and between state institutions there may be many competing voices. States base their policies of control and prohibition of drugs on a set of assumptions: everyone wants to try drugs; if they try them they will become addicted; addiction corrupts the individual and society and could ultimately destroy the state. This view is encapsulated by George W. Bush: 'we must reduce drug use for one great moral reason: over time, drugs rob men, women and children of their dignity, and their character. Illegal drugs are enemies of ambition and hope. When we fight against drugs we fight for the souls of our fellow Americans' (cit. Federal Drug Control Programs, 2003, 376). States also assume that if drugs are illegal people will not try them, or that those who do will be few enough to be manageable. This prompts states to prohibit what are described as 'dangerous drugs', dangerous not necessarily in the sense of killing the user, although sometimes this does happen, but dangerous in the sense that drugs cause degeneration of the individual and endanger social cohesion and the stability of the state. The signatories to the UN Single Convention on Narcotic Drugs (1961) recognized 'that addiction to narcotic drugs constitutes a serous evil for the individual and is fraught with social and economic danger to mankind'. In Britain these sentiments are reflected in the key piece of anti-drug

16

legislation, the 1971 Misuse of Drugs Act, which refers to drugs having 'harmful effects sufficient to constitute a social problem'. Little wonder then that drug prohibition is enforced with the full coercive powers at states' disposal: fines; asset seizure, imprisonment and even capital punishment. In August 2009, for example, Iran hanged 24 convicted drug traffickers. Two months earlier, on what the UN has declared to be International Day Against Drug Abuse and Trafficking (26 June), China demonstrated its commitment to prohibition by executing six convicted traffickers by firing squad. States reinforce these deterrent measures by providing drugs education to persuade young people to 'just say no' and hopefully to frighten potential users from trying drugs by highlighting the cases of drug deaths and the health risks to the user. They use propaganda to popularize the idea that drugs are evil. In America, in the aftermath of 9/11, President George W. Bush warned drug users that by buying drugs they were supporting America's enemies who used drug money to perpetrate terrorism: 'If you quit drugs, you join the fight against terrorism in America' (cit. Campbell, 2002). Making a clear link between the war on drugs and the war on terror, the US Office of National Drug Control Policy ran an advertising campaign warning that Americans who buy drugs may be financing terrorists. In addition to this repertoire of domestic policies, states also use narco-diplomacy to persuade other states to cooperate in bilateral and multinational prohibition agreements and strategies against the drug trade.

We might question the validity of some of the assumptions that underpin this kind of drug policy. Does everyone want to try drugs? Would they if they were legal? Does trying, or even regularly using, drugs always lead to addiction? These questions are hard to answer, but one could reasonably suppose the answers would be negative. For states such speculation is irrelevant; a drug-free-for-all in which anyone could use any drugs they wished is just too risky.

The drug problem for states concerns not just what is but what might be. Nineteenth-century China provides a cautionary tale. Opium has had a long history in China where it has been used medicinally at least since the thirteenth century, but the introduction of tobacco in the seventeenth century led to the recreational practice of opium smoking. Initially, this habit was confined to the rich but by the eighteenth century the problems associated with opium smoking were becoming apparent as the habit became increasingly widespread. Work and family were neglected for opium. By 1729, prompted by the social side effects, an imperial edict prohibited the practice, but, as we have come to recognize as normal with prohibitions, it was almost impossible to enforce and widely ignored. It was followed by two further edicts, in 1796 and 1799, banning imports of opium, which were also ignored. In 1839 China had its own 'Boston tea party' of sorts when Emperor Daoguang had a consignment of opium, consisting of approximately 20,000 chests, seized and destroyed on the beach in full public view. As a result China became embroiled in the first drugs wars, the Opium Wars of 1839–42 and 1856–60, against the lucrative opium trade which was dominated by the British, in particular the British East India Company. On both of these occasions China was defeated. In the latter half of the nineteenth century China's Manchu dynasty was disintegrating. It was unable to maintain its territorial integrity in the face of British, French, Japanese, German and Russian attempts to penetrate its economy and annex its territory. Opium addiction was a widespread and growing problem. By this time China had an estimated 40 million opium addicts (see Yang-wen, 2001, chap. 10). By the end of the nineteenth century China's inability to maintain its sovereignty under threat from the imperialist economies of Europe, led to much searching for someone or something to blame. Opium was identified as the enemy; it came to be seen as the main source of China's ills. Reformers blamed China's problems on its backwardness, which was symbolized by opium smoking and foot binding. Zheng Guang thought that 'the poppy destroyed agriculture, impoverished the commoner, depraved the official and weakened the farmer and he depicted opium as a 'natural disaster' and chronic illness undermining the nation' (cit. Dikötter et al., 2004, 108). In sentiments that continue to inform today's international drug war, opium was depicted as a product forced upon China by foreigners who were intent upon weakening its population and undermining its culture and economy. 'Peddled by imperialist powers, insinuating itself into the blood stream of the nation, poisoning the minds and bodies of the country's millions, opium gradually emerged as a symbol of national weakness.' (cit. Dikötter et al., 2004, 109). By the turn of the century China itself seemed to have adopted an 'If you can't beat 'em join 'em' policy, the opium ban was lifted and China became a leading producer of the drug. But by this time the Europeans were becoming less enamoured of a drugs trade that was clearly lucrative, but which was rapidly coming to be seen as morally reprehensible. The Americans were shocked by tales brought home by returning missionaries, who described the terrible effects that opium was having on families in China. A coincidence of increasing knowledge about the addictive effects of opium and its derivatives (morphine and heroin) and the example of China in the grip of opium addiction, stiffened the resolve for 'something to be done' about the issue of drugs. American initiatives led to the creation of the first international drug forum in 1909 in Shanghai. This was quickly followed by a prohibition agreement in The Hague in 1912.

China was a relatively recent example that could be used in support of the need for drug prohibition. But the idea that drugs are bad for the individual and bad for the state, long pre-dated the modern period. Western civilization is underpinned by a set of beliefs about the good life, the good citizen and the well-ordered state, and we inherited much of this from the Ancient Greeks.

The Greek city-states of the fifth and fourth centuries BC existed for the common defence and the achievement of excellence. Citizens should be able to fulfil their human potential. The emergence of the modern democratizing state in nineteenth- and twentieth-century Europe led citizens to expect something similar. They expect not only defence from attack from outside and the upholding of law and order within, but also that the state should deliver an extensive range of economic and welfare benefits, to put a good life within everybody's reach. The justifications for drug control evolved to encompass not only ideas about the wickedness of drugs and their destructive effect on the individual, but also to empirical arguments centring on the negative economic, social and political impact of drugs. It is to these ideological, economic, social and political explanations for prohibition that we now turn.

Ideological explanations for prohibition

Ideological explanations for the prohibition of drugs focus on the idea that drugs are wicked and that using them is morally wrong. Ideas such as these can be traced back to the beginning of western civilization. These ideas are underpinned by a set of beliefs about the effects of drugs on human behaviour and the knock-on effect this has had on society. Drugs are seductive and addictive. Experimenting with drug use leads to addiction, an altered state of being in which the individual's craving for drugs supersedes all other responsibilities, relationships and interests, including even neglecting their own personal health, hygiene and nourishment. Of course, governments know that not all users will become addicts, but the chance that they will is too risky.

Drugs are evil. Drugs are a question of morality. It was noted in the previous chapter that the term 'drug' implies disapproval. It creates a sense of unease that centres on the conflict between what it is to be human and to lead a full life, and the narrow, obsessive life of an addict. This belief that drug use is morally wrong leads to the conclusion that it should be prohibited. Drugs are sinful; there can be no room for compromise. Drug prohibition is a moral imperative. It is this kind of belief that informs the American approach to drugs that America has successfully internationalized. In the 1961 UN Single Convention, referred to above, the signatories note that they are 'conscious of their *duty* to prevent and combat this evil [narcotic drugs]' (my emphasis). In an essay defending the prohibition of drugs, the American academic and former chairman of the National Advisory Commission on Drug Abuse Prevention (1971–3), James Q. Wilson makes the point clear when he famously compares the damage caused by tobacco with that caused by cocaine: 'Tobacco shortens one's life, cocaine debases it. Nicotine alters one's habits, cocaine alters one's soul' (Wilson, 1990, 40).

Drugs corrupt the individual and undermine society. Drugs may enable us to cast off the veneer of civilization. Western civilization may have begun with Homer, and it is Homer who also tells us what drugs can do to civilization. Odysseus recounts how, only nine days after leaving Troy, his ship is blown off-course to an unknown land. He sends three men ashore to investigate, and they try the local fruit, the lotus. 'A single taste of this native fruit made my soldiers forget everything they had ever known: where they were from, where they were going, everything.' He goes on to say, 'although many of my other men would have enjoyed this easy way of living . . . I decided I wouldn't give them the chance to choose it. For their own good, of course.' He realizes that the three who had tasted the drug would not give up the lotus willingly, therefore he puts them in chains in the hold of the ship and quickly sets sail before any more of the ship's people can fall under the spell of this dangerous fruit (*The Odyssey*, book 9).

This passage from Homer evokes several of our own common attitudes to drugs. Drugs are dangerously seductive and almost always addictive. They promise an easier life, an alternative to end-driven life rooted in moral and social codes. Once we have taken drugs, it is as if we become sick and choose to remain sick. Drugs lead us to lose our sense of reality and responsibility. Sickness and health lose their ordinary meanings. Drug users come to believe that they are in a better condition than non-users. The sickness of drug taking also brings with it the threat of contagion. Non-users are likely to be tempted to join users in their alternative world; hence we attempt to isolate drug users. We treat them as outcasts and dismiss them as junkies. We introduce prohibition to reinforce the will of the non-user. Users will, at best, be seen as sick, or as deviants, or even as sociopaths. Authority's job is to stop users and potential users 'for their own good' and to force detoxification and rehabilitation on those who have succumbed to temptation. In some countries, in the name of curing them, drug addicts are literally put in chains, like Odysseus' men (see Human Rights Watch, 2003). It is also from the *Odyssey* that we learn that some drugs are acceptable while others are not. Odysseus is concerned about the corrupting effects of the lotus, a drug which is alien and new. But with little comment, in book 4, there is an account of Helen of Troy administering a drug to Menelaus, Nestor and Telemachus when they are overcome with sadness on the eve of departure to search for the long-lost Odysseus: 'Into the wine they were drinking she cast a drug which melted sorrow and sweetened gall, which made men forgetful of their pains.' We are told that this drug is so strong that no matter what appalling fate became a man's family, he would not cry that day. The identity of this drug has been a matter for speculation but a common contemporary assumption is that it was opium.

Homer had already stirred up fears about the dangers of drugs long before Plato and Aristotle laid the basis of our conception of citizenship and the good life, and those negative conceptions still inform the way we think about drug use. In *The Republic*, Plato describes the just state and the just individual. According to him, individuals are just when they are internally well ordered, their passions and appetites being ruled by reason. Plato's city is largely composed of those who are ruled by the passions or appetites, people suited to be warriors or farmers and craftsmen. They will be ruled by men and women in whom reason rules. Each class contributes what it can to the city, and the resulting harmony is justice. Such a city would have no place for a drug user. Drug users are not even ruled by appetites in general, but by a single, overwhelming appetite. They would not toil, neither would they spin. They would be unharmonious, parasites, an anti-social menace. This kind of view still informs modern attitudes to drug users. It is reflected clearly in headlines such as '350,000 Heroin and Crack Addicts Claim a Staggering £1.6 bn in Benefits' (*Daily Mail*, 21 August 2009).

It is Aristotle who taught us what it means to say 'Man is a political animal'. Nature intends that men should live in a properly constituted city-state, a classical polis. We cannot be fully human unless we live good lives in societies that are well ordered by laws. This good life is to be lived in the pursuit of a multiplicity of ends, and this the drug user cannot – or will not – do. Drugs make the user unfit for the Aristotelian good life. The drug user is an outlaw who has no place in the city; in the city he is a dangerous parasite. Further, drug use often becomes addiction, a state of mind which can be wildly anti-social. The desire for drugs becomes the user's single end, the antithesis of everything for which the good life stands.

Drugs can threaten the stability and safety of the state. Authority is haunted by the fear of the emergence of a heroin republic, a state within the state, in which social responsibility, the work ethic and the work of building civilization give way to instant gratification through drug-induced euphoria. In this state people ignore all social norms to concentrate on their next fix. Children are born addicts, family life is neglected, and children grow up without positive role models. It would be a state in which a semi-anaesthetised majority lives off the work of the few.

But this spectre of the heroin republic does not haunt everyone. For the amoral, the moral relativists and the sceptics, a range of other rationales for prohibition are offered. The 1961 UN Single Convention on Narcotic Drugs refers not only to drugs being a serious *evil* for the individual but also claims that drugs are 'fraught with social and economic danger to mankind'. It is to economic explanations for drug prohibition that we now turn.

Economic explanations for prohibition

Drugs may be evil and immoral. They may be an obstacle to achieving the Aristotelian good life. They may threaten the stability of the state and even the life everlasting of the immortal soul, but the downside of the supply and use of drugs from an economic perspective is much less clear-cut. Drugs have economic costs but they also bring economic benefits and it is partly because of such benefits that drug prohibition is brought into disrepute. When America, aided and abetted by other powerful states in Western Europe, pushed for the internationalization of prohibition, the proposed ban did not encompass all psycho-active substances. Those psychoactive substances in which they had considerable economic interests, alcohol and tobacco, where not prohibited as drugs, although the USA did have a period (14 years) of alcohol prohibition. This section will examine some of contradictions that have made drug policy difficult to explain on moral grounds alone, and which require an appreciation of an underlying economic rationale.

Most states have signed up to the three UN Conventions (1961, 1971 and 1988) prohibiting the cultivation, manufacture, trafficking and dealing of a long list of psychoactive substances that many people want to use recreationally. But there is ambivalence about the economic benefits attached to drugs which raises questions about their prohibition. One of those questions that tend to baffle some of us centres on the inconsistent nature of prohibition. Caffeine is a psychoactive substance that is unregulated and legal; tobacco and alcohol are psychoactive substances which are regulated and legal, whilst cannabis and ecstasy, for example, are banned. Yet in terms of danger or harm there is not a lot to choose between them.

Caffeine is possibly the most widely used psychoactive substance in the world with its use being neither prohibited nor regulated. It is the active ingredient of tea, coffee, chocolate, soft drinks and energy supplements. Philip Robson, a consultant psychiatrist, describes caffeine as 'a highly addictive stimulant associated with physical and psychological withdrawal symptoms' if use is stopped abruptly (Robson, 2009, 1). He goes on to emphasize that caffeine has toxic effects and that it can be overdosed (ibid., 1). Coffee is one of the most popular ways of consuming caffeine. When it was first imported to Europe from the Ottoman Empire it was not welcomed by everyone. It was seen as a Muslim drink and there were calls for its prohibition. In England, in 1674, there was even a 'Women's Petition Against Coffee' which blamed coffee for male impotence. Coffee was described as an 'Abominable, Heathenish Liquor... which Riffling Nature of her Choicest Treasure, and Drying up the Radical moisture, has so eunucht our Husbands, and Crippled our more kind Gallants, that they are become as Impotent, as Age, and as unfruitful as those Desarts whence that unhappy Berry is said to be brought' (Women's Petition against Coffee 1674). But as the 'foreignness' of coffee began to recede its usefulness became more apparent. Not only was it a profitable trading commodity but it also brought other economic benefits. The caffeine in coffee helped people to concentrate, enabling them to work harder for longer. Employers soon recognized the value of incorporating coffee and tea breaks into the working day. Eventually coffee was not only accepted but its use has become actively encouraged.

Tobacco has already been discussed in chapter 2, where it was compared with coca and its derivatives. Despite its legal status, today's tobacco smokers are under siege. In Britain we see them huddled outside shops, offices and pubs, in the cold and damp, puffing away, engaged in what has come to be seen as an anti-social habit. They are bombarded with anti-smoking propaganda. Even packets of cigarettes now not only inform smokers that smoking kills, they also include lurid pictures of arteries and lungs clogged with tar deposits. The smoking habit, we are told, not only endangers the health not only the smoker, but also the health of those around them through 'passive smoking'. Yet it was not so many years ago that cigarette adverts were everywhere: on billboards, on television, in films and all over the sporting events sponsored by cigarette manufacturers. In both world wars the troops were treated to cigarettes. Cigarette smoking was something to be encouraged. Nicotine was an aid to concentration and simultaneously pacified the smoker. Although smoking has now become less acceptable and labelled anti-social, it remains legal and makes a considerable contribution to international trade and national exchequers. In America, for example, annual tobacco sales exceed $45 billion, the tobacco industry provides 50,000 manufacturing jobs, about 136,000 farming jobs directly plus a further 400,000 jobs indirectly. Over a ten-year period the US Treasury is estimated to have pocketed $118.6 billion in tobacco taxes. The UK does not grow tobacco but it still benefits hugely from the tobacco industry which employs about 9,000 people and supports about 139,000 other jobs (BBC News, 28 September 1999). In terms of tax revenue, in 2006–7 tobacco contributed approximately £10 billion to the British Treasury (www.the-tma.org.uk/tobacco-tax-revenue.aspx). Matthew Norman, writing in the *Independent*, argues that 'Smokers should be praised not banned' because 'they contribute many billions more to the economy than they take in healthcare' (Norman, 2009). In the USA, the industry's website, Tobacco Working for America, describes the effects of tobacco as 'like the ripples from a stone thrown in a lake, the activities of the tobacco industry create waves of economic benefits that flow continuously into almost every segment of the American economy'. It also highlights tobacco's role as a cash crop: 'at over $4000 per acre, tobacco is clearly a valuable cash crop – exceeding the combined dollar value per acre for such leading cash crops as wheat, hay, soy beans, corn, cotton, peanuts and tree nuts' (http://fujipub.com/fot/working.html). These are sentiments echoed by the *cocaleros* of the Andes and the poppy farmers of Afghanistan in respect of their own psychoactive crops.

Alcohol is a psychoactive substance that is widely used and accepted in the West and most of the world. A visit to almost any present-day British town on a Friday and Saturday night, and perhaps on any night of the week, might raise a question or two about the role alcohol plays in public order problems. There are frequent drunken brawls and a good deal of obnoxious and often threatening behaviour from people tanked up on alcohol. On top of this there are a lot of other anti-social goings-on, including vomiting and urinating in shop doorways and alleys. It is hardly surprising that some people question the wisdom of 24-hour pub opening, cheap supermarket booze and alcohol on sale in motorway service stations the length and breadth of the country. Terry Kirby believes that 'despite intensive public health campaigns, alcohol sales have risen ... while alcohol is at least 65% more affordable than it was in 1980. Doctors, senior policy officers and charities are calling on the government to act' (Kirby, 2009). In New Zealand the Alcohol Action Group has gone so far as to claim that supermarkets are drug pushers and that the selling of high quantities of discounted wines 'should be viewed the same as dealers dishing out ecstasy pills or morphine' (Vass, 2010).

For those in authority, uncomfortable comparisons can always be drawn between the aggressive, loutish behaviour linked to alcohol use and the behaviour of those who use cannabis or even the class A drug, ecstasy (see Travis, 2009). Cannabis users tend to smoke a joint and become relaxed, giggly and hungry (in street slang 'getting the munchies'). It is hard to recognise the average cannabis user in the lurid descriptions offered by Harry Anslinger (the US Commissioner on Narcotics 1950s) lurid descriptions:

> Marijuana (cannabis) is only and always a scourge which undermines its victims and degrades them mentally, morally and physically ... a small dose ... may bring about intense intoxication, raving fits and criminal assaults... It is the unpredictable effect which makes marijuana one of the most dangerous drugs known... the moral barricades are broken down and often debauchery and sexuality results. (Anslinger, 1937)

Anslinger's description seems to be far more applicable to the drunk than to the stoned.

Ecstasy, a stimulant whose main ingredient is MDMA (methylenedioxymethamphetamine), is said to make individuals feel 'loved up'. Clubbers say that it gives them the energy to dance all night, makes them love the world and feel themselves to be loved by it in return. After all-night clubbing on ecstasy most users simply sleep it off (see Harris, 2009). They do not inflict boorish, loutish behaviour on those around them as is frequently the case with drunks. This is not to say that cannabis and ecstasy have no downside for individual users. In Britain many recall the unfortunate Leah Betts who died after one dose of ecstasy, and recently much more has been made of links between cannabis use and psychosis (see, for instance, Dr Philip Robson, 'Cannabis and Psychosis, Panorama, BBC, 19 June 2005; Christopher Hope, 'Cannabis "Can Cause Psychosis in Healthy People"', *Telegraph*, 27 July 2009; BBC News, 'Skunk Bigger Psychosis Risk', 2009; Hall and Degenhardt 2011).

These comparisons between the legal awfulness of alcohol and illegal cannabis and ecstasy do make prohibition difficult to explain. But alcohol is big business, playing a key role in the economy in terms of profits to the makers of drinks, salaries to employees of the drinks manufacturers and trade, and taxes for the exchequer. In Britain the alcohol industry alone employs 980,000 people in the production and retailing side and if indirect jobs are included, over 1.8 million jobs. It contributes £21 billion in gross domestic product (Oxford Economic Outlook for the UK Drinks Sector Report 2010). Multiply that across much of the globe and it is easy to see why its legal status seems untouchable.

In Muslim countries, of course, alcohol is strictly forbidden. The use of alcohol is often severely (from a western perspective) punished such as in Saudi Arabia where alcohol use is punishable by public flogging. But in these countries prohibition is deeply embedded in, and reinforced by, religious beliefs. Even in the West alcohol has long provoked ambivalence. As far back as Ancient Greece, Plato and Socrates drew attention to 'the darker side of alcohol' including its association with public disorder and violence. It caused men to neglect their families and their work (Robson, 2009. 31).

In Britain alcohol, in the form of ale, has been the native drink since at least Roman times. It was drunk by people of all ages and classes, being considered safer than water. It was not until the eighteenth century that concerns about alcohol became pressing. This change in attitude was prompted by two things: spirits became accessible to the lower classes and industrialization changed the nature of work. Philip Robins notes that 'until around 1700 restrictive practices ensured consumption of distilled drinks in Britain was almost entirely confined to the wealthy' but the 'cancellation of the monopoly hitherto enjoyed by the Worshipful Company of Distillers led to the infamous "gin craze" among the poor' (Robson, 2009, 33). Hogarth's Gin Lane illustrates the social effects of the unregulated use of strong spirits. Prudence and morality disappear into a bottle of gin, and children and work are neglected as all sense of duty succumbs to drunkenness. Spirits brought 'starving, ragged children and weeping bruised wives with empty pantries' (Bancroft, 2009, 21). Industrialization made the need for control of alcohol more urgent. A drunken labourer could do little damage in the pre-machine age, but the coming of the mechanized factory provided an economic motive for the regulation of drink. The drunken worker could be a menace in the machine age. British governments responded to the Gin Craze by prohibiting gin, but, finding the nation's drinking habits made this impossible, resorted to regulation instead. Bancroft claims that it was the Gin Craze that ushered in this 'new kind of culturally and economically determined drunkenness' (ibid., 28).

The British government's failure to enforce prohibition of spirits in the eighteenth century did not deter the Americans from trying to do the same 200 years later, or for that matter the Icelanders, the Finns and the Russians trying to do so as well. Prohibition of alcohol in America, dubbed 'the Noble Experiment' by Congress (Kleinman, 2006), lasted only 14 years (1917–31), but this was long enough for it to prove itself unworkable and a cause of increased criminal behaviour. Julia Buxton remarks that 'alcohol prohibition in America was a specific response to the unique tensions generated by the economic modernization process' (Buxton, 2006, 20) and that it was 'fuelled by religious and ideological values of the period and inspired by an idealized vision of the American nation' (ibid.). Drunkenness, and in particular drunkenness blamed, not on locally brewed cider or corn liquor, but on the imported 'demon rum', was ungodly and un-American, which was much the same thing, and was incompatible with the demands of factory work in an industrialized economy. Prohibition soon proved itself to be unworkable, even though it had been introduced through the highest law of the land by the 18th Amendment to the Constitution in 1917. The criminalization of private acts did not stop them happening (Buxton, 2006, 25), but it did lead to the widespread corruption of officials and it caused a huge growth of organized crime. Bootleggers were determined to supply the lucrative liquor trade with imported booze for those able to afford it, and they were willing to use violence in pursuit of their profits. The less well-off had to settle for moonshine and bath tub gin, some of which was lethal.

Alcohol prohibition, except where it is linked with high levels of religious observance, has proved itself unworkable, and – from an economic perspective – undesirable. It may be thought wicked and harmful by some, it may cause work days to be lost and impose health costs, but it mediates these costs by being hugely popular and a cash cow for the taxman. Melanie Reid observes that

> we have been guilty of dancing to a totally phoney moral tune for centuries about alcohol ... We sustain breathtaking double standards about criticising alcohol consumption while encouraging it for revenue and social control. Hogarth's scenes of the horrors of Gin Lane speak of nothing we are not familiar with today, of a populace kept in its place and yet destroyed by alcohol. The oldest

edict of power in the land: intoxicate the masses and keep them malleable. (Reid, 2009b)

By the middle of the nineteenth century these concerns about the impact of alcohol on the productivity of workers were easily extended to the impact of what were becoming widely available and abused opiate and cocaine preparations. But even these drugs have economic benefits. After having conducted research into the problems of the Afghan economy as far back as 1989, Guy Brailsford noted that 'were it not for the undesirability of the end product, opium cultivation would be considered the ideal solution to the agricultural problems of Badakstan, and aid agencies would no doubt be heartily promoting its cultivation' (Brailsford, 1989). Twenty years on, these comments are equally applicable to the role that opium plays in the economy of Afghanistan. Afghanistan is now the source of 90 per cent of the world's illegal opium crop that ends up as heroin on European streets. Opium has been grown and smoked in small quantities in Afghanistan for centuries. It was in the wake of the 1979 Soviet invasion that it began to replace traditional crops. On the one hand the Soviet forces, as part of a 'scorched earth' policy designed to deny the mujahideen cover and local support, destroyed the qanat, the centuries-old irrigation system, on which the traditional fruit crops and vegetables relied (Burke, 2004). On the other hand, the Central Intelligence Agency (CIA) and the Pakistani Inter Service Intelligence (ISI), provided encouragement, or at the very least turned a blind eye, when the mujahideen funded their insurgency against the Soviet invaders by opium production (Misra, 2004, 131–3). This demonstrates the ambivalence of authorities. When faced with competing priorities, in this case the West's anxiety about imperialist intentions of the Cold War enemy, authorities have been willing to reap the economic benefits from drugs despite the ideological arguments against doing so.

This kind of ambivalence about the economic value of drugs is not confined to the late twentieth century – and nor is it confined to the case of opium. The chewing of coca leaves has been part of everyday life in the Andes for thousands of years, being used medicinally, recreationally and in sacred ceremonies. It was even used as a medium of exchange. When the Spanish conquistadors conquered the Inca Empire in 1572 they banned the use of coca leaf. Its pagan associations were considered to be incompatible with Roman Catholicism and anyway, to the incomers, it was an unknown, foreign substance and therefore a potential threat. In common with most prohibitions, this one failed, use continued and the conquistadors were soon impressed by coca's stimulant effects. They noted that the herb was so nutritious and invigorating that the Indians who chewed it could work harder and for longer and with little or no food. It was particularly useful in the gruelling conditions of the silver mines. The chewing of coca reduced the appetite and increased the stamina of the miners. Soon, not only was the ban lifted, but the native workers were encouraged to use coca and were even paid in it.

Coca remains a bone of contention to the present day. Two of the key producing countries, Peru and Bolivia, have indigenous populations who continue to chew coca and use a wide variety of products containing it, despite the international prohibition of coca that came into force in the late 1980s. It was prohibited under the 1961 UN Convention, but traditional users were granted a 25-year transition period to bring the prohibition into force. 'Coca Yes, Cocaine No' has become their slogan. They claim that their use of coca is comparable with the use of caffeine in tea and coffee around the world and that its prohibition infringes their human rights. But coca is the basis of cocaine and crack, and these are regarded as evil in the USA and Europe, the main markets for the consumption of drugs, although clearly many of the citizens across the USA and Europe do not agree with this view because cocaine is rapidly becoming the most popular drug of choice after cannabis (Campbell, 2009). It comes as no surprise that it is the USA that is leading, successfully so far, the opposition to the 'Coca Yes' campaign in the UNODC.

There have been a number of cost–benefit analyses of the role of coca in the economies of Colombia, Peru and Bolivia (see, for example, Clawson and Lee III 1998). However, the obstacles in the way of trying to measure the effects of a semi-covert activity and the difficulty of quantifying the costs of the anti-drugs policies and the impact of interventions on the quality of life of the ordinary people involved, give rise to many uncertainties. Some of these costs and consequences of prohibition will be discussed more fully in chapter 5. For the present, suffice it to say that coca is a highly lucrative cash crop for which there is a steady illegal market. It is relatively easy to cultivate because it tolerates a wide variety of soil types, climate and topography. It is disease-resistant, high yield and stores well. It has a high value to weight ratio and can bear the cost of transportation from inaccessible areas, with poor infrastructures, such as exist in much of the Andes, to distant markets. It is labour intensive and therefore helps to alleviate rural poverty and unemployment. The positive multiplier effect it has on the wider economy, mirroring the claims made for tobacco in America and Britain noted above, means that the socio-economic influence of the coca crop extends beyond the farmers to the wider community and national economy. It is no surprise that there is a good deal of resentment about prohibition in countries which have a long tradition of coca use and for which it has now become a valuable cash crop. Evo Morales, a former coca farmer elected president of Bolivia in 2005, showed his own contempt for the UN's prohibition of coca when, earlier this year (12 March 2009) he made his point by chewing coca while addressing the delegates at the UNODC.

On top of all this there is yet another economic perspective to the drugs question, that of the ghetto economy. In the user countries the low-level street corner drugs economy has become a thriving source of employment and identity for many young people who have few or no other prospects. Mike Collison points out that drugs give such youngsters 'something to do, places to go, deals to make, arrests to evade, status to maintain. Local organizations that distribute drugs have become, in many communities, important sources of wealth and social status' (Collison, 1996). It is worth noting that the downturn in the industrial economies in Europe in the 1980s coincided with a dramatic upsurge in drug use and in the drug economies. By the 1990s the drug economy had become a central feature of the depressed areas in large American cities. It attracts young, unemployed black and Latino youths, reinforcing once again the link between race and drugs. It provides a lucrative income and Bruce Bullington explains how they see the work as 'exciting, interesting and allows for considerable free time in which to enjoy the fruits of their labors' (Bullington, 1998, 124). It can be seen as a money transfer system in which poor, unemployed youths in deprived urban areas help the rich, more privileged young people to dispose of their income, which is transferred to those with the highest propensity to consume. This too has a multiplier effect throughout the community, and in the wider national economy.

There may be another, less obvious economic explanation for drug prohibition. Shane Blackman, for example, argues that 'the US militarization of the "drug war" provides a cover for foreign policy intervention into other states to exert American influence and create opportunities for corporate capital' (Blackman, 2004, 3). He claims that US policy is 'presented as being liberal or benevolent when in fact the 'drug war' acts as a cover for pursuit of economic and political interest' (ibid., 28). The drug war can act as a cover for the pursuit of other unrelated foreign policy ends. Certainly US leadership of the internationalization of drug control in 1909 may have had a moral cause, but this did not preclude economic motives. The US expected to be a beneficiary of the opening up of trade with China as a result of 'sucking up' to China in its anti-opium trade fight against the old great powers of Europe (McAllister, 2000, 31; Buxton, 2006, 139).

Economic arguments in favour of drug prohibition usually have little to say about the economic benefits that accrue to those powerful nations that were able to determine which list of psychoactive substances would be banned. Instead, emphasis is placed on the economic costs imposed by drugs. The heroin user, who nods off when he has had his fix and becomes agitated, anxious and perhaps aggressive when he is withdrawing, is not a good employment prospect. The UNDCP (the UN drugs and crime programme, previously called UNODC) report into the social impact of drugs claims that 'Work tasks that require a higher level of judgement, constant alterations, immediate memory and fine motor skills are easily disrupted by drugs … Drug abusers have more absenteeism, accidents on the job, medical claims and lost production than non-users' (UNDCP 1995). Even if employers are willing to give addicts a chance, business insurance companies would be unlikely to extend cover to cover them. David Courtwright summarizes the position as follows: 'theft, accidents and legal liability give employers every incentive to avoid illicit drug users and urine tests give them the means of their detection' (Courtwright, 2001, 200). It is this kind of scenario that adds grist to the mill of those who raise economic arguments against drugs. Drugs create addicts; addicts become a non-productive burden on the economy, and in the modern welfare state, a drain on everyone else. Drugs, therefore, pose an economic threat because they may lead to the dreaded 'heroin republic' in which idle addicts outnumber workers. Those who argue that the work days lost because of alcohol are an even greater burden on the economy, can simply be refuted by accepting that, yes, alcohol is a problem so why, just for the sake of consistency, make everything much worse by legalizing a range of other intoxicants that are equally or more problematic?

Drugs are not simply a drain on economic sources; they also bring economic benefits. The notion that one country's drug is another country's cash crop exposes the current prohibition regime as something rich, powerful countries have been able to impose on weaker countries, to ensure that only those drugs largely controlled by, used by and approved by the powerful remain legal. The economic arguments for prohibition are equivocal. Perhaps the social dangers of drugs offer more convincing argument for prohibition.

Sociological explanations for prohibition

The social dangers that supposedly attach to drug use centre on the breakdown of families, the neglect of children and the destruction of communities. But once again all of these outcomes apply as much to the use of legal as to illegal psychoactive substances. Social explanations in support of prohibition reflect less on what drugs actually do to social cohesion and more on the power and effectiveness of those pressure groups which want to ban drugs. The greater social dangers associated with drugs, including systemic violence, acquisitive crime, health costs and the destruction of amenities in the community, arise more from the illegal status of drugs than from any inherent harm they may cause. International prohibition excludes the drugs acceptable to, and profitable for, the rich and powerful countries in the world. These countries have succeeded in imposing their preferences on what is loosely referred to as the 'international community'. But these preferences also reflect the success of particular pressure groups within the rich and powerful countries. This is not to deny that drugs can damage people and communities, but it is to claim that it is only when powerful groups identify these effects as a cause for moral panic that authorities are galvanized into action.

Most people use psychoactive substances. Some need a strong cup of coffee to start the day, others require nicotine from that first cigarette and some need heroin to be able to function. Authorities have no interest in the coffee drinker, they have developed an interest in the cigarette smoker and their interest in the heroin user is already well established. One of the social triggers that led to a call for the state to interest itself in these matters is the use of a drug spreading from being a recreation for the elite and percolates to the masses or at least the lower classes. When Helen of Troy administers a drug to King Menelaus and his friends, it arouses no comment, but when three of Odysseus's ship's people, the rank and file, taste the lotus it is a cause for concern and consternation. Its use will be contagious and its effects threaten the destruction of morals and social responsibility.

While opium smoking in China was confined to the rich it was not regarded as a problem. When opium smoking spreads to the lower classes it becomes a political issue. It also becomes a useful scapegoat for elite failure. It is when the Manchu dynasty can no longer hold the line in the face of foreign economic and territorial penetration that opium smoking is prohibited. It is depicted as the cause of China's weaknesses: workers would rather smoke opium than work; farmers would rather grow opium than grow food.

A similar pattern can be found in the gin-crazed Britain of the eighteenth century. Spirits were not considered to be a problem when they were only available to the wealthy. It was when cheap gin became everyone's and anyone's tipple that the clamour for control began. The government was called upon to act and prohibition was the result. But prohibition was impossible to enforce and it created a further set of social problems. The gin industry to the masses was handed over to organized crime and this had a devastating effect on the health of gin drinkers (Dillon, 2002). In the end the government opted for regulation, allowing social mores to develop to internalize control on the way people drink, for example, only drinking in the evening, after work, only social drinking, drinking in pubs, places that have been identified as the socially acceptable venues for drinking alcohol. The perceived failure of younger generations to observe these customs has given rise to what is now described as Britain's 'binge drinking' culture and again cries are being raised that something should be done. But in contrast to illegal drugs, alcohol has a firmly entrenched position both in society and in the economy. It is not alcohol that is blamed for public disorder, family breakdown, domestic violence, work days lost and the increasing number of alcohol-related health problems; it is the failure to observe the drinking codes. The source of the problem is identified as a younger generation who drink for oblivion, aided and abetted by supermarkets selling cheap booze. This has resulted in everyone being bombarded with messages about the health risks associated with the way they drink. The message is 'If you drink, drink responsibly': an exhortation to observe the codes. This message is reinforced by warnings to those who sell cheap alcohol that they must do a better job of policing the alcohol laws that prohibit its sale to under-18s. They are also under pressure to increase their prices, and there are demands for prohibition of alcohol adverts (see, for example, Jack, 2009). However, alcohol is big business, and already those protecting the alcohol industry have been stirred into counter-measures. The Scottish government's recent proposal to tackle Scotland's alcohol problem has been attacked by American drinks companies who have urged ministers to abandon this policy. Tom Peterkin says that 'The Distilled Spirits Council of the United States has warned that the controversial policy may contravene international rules and will affect trade' and that the Scottish Whisky Association are claiming that '"price controls are likely to break EU and international trade law" and that the Scottish Government seems to be intent on giving the green light to countries to introduce health-based restriction against Scottish whisky, undermining exports and Scottish jobs' (Peterkin, 2009). In March 2011, the British government's much-trumpeted 'responsibility deal' negotiated with the drinks industry, covering issues such as cheap drink promotions and labelling, and aimed at tackling alcohol abuse, was rejected by health groups. Alcohol Concern described it as 'all carrot and no stick for the drinks industry and supermarkets'. It accused the government of allowing the drinks industry to propose half-hearted pledges on alcohol. Alcohol Concern's chief executive, Don Shenker, claimed the government 'clearly shows that when it comes to public health, its first priority is to side with big business and protect private profit'. These views were endorsed by the British Association for the Study of the Liver, the British Liver Trust, the British Medical Association, the Institute of Alcohol Studies and the Royal College of Physicians (BBC News, 14 March 2011).

The class-linked association between drug use and control can also be identified in relation to the treatment of what we now call class A drugs, cocaine and heroin. If a new kind of drunkenness was publicly defined in the eighteenth century, 'drugs' are an invention of the end of the nineteenth and start of the twentieth century. It is not until then that cocaine and opiates come to be identified as threats. Both were used widely for medical purposes and were readily available in patent medicines. Recreational use was mostly confined to the upper classes and the literati. When Thomas de Quincey bemoans the indolent life of the opium eater who almost exclusively desires intoxication, it is of no great concern. What is the problem with using a little opium if the result is Coleridge's 'Kubla Khan'? Does it matter if Sigmund Freud not only uses cocaine but also writes articles in the medical press about this wonderful substance, and recommends it to, and acquires it for, his friends? It is a different matter when the use of cocaine and opiates in patent medicines begins to give the masses a taste for the fringe benefits of these substances: the reduction of psychological pain, a temporary sense of well-being, a sense of invulnerability, excitement, in short a different, chemically induced, alternative to a life that is nasty, brutish and short. It was the 1916 Defence of the Realm Act (DORA, section 40b) that introduced drug prohibition in Britain. Soldiers returning on leave from the front-line were being introduced to the delights of cocaine, which could easily undermine the fighting spirit of the troops. It gave the media a field day highlighting the dangers of cocaine, and henceforth the possession of cocaine and opiates, without medical authorization, became illegal.

Britain went along with the internationalization of drug control. Its representatives attended the Shanghai Opium Commission and it signed up to promising prohibition in The Hague 1912 Opium Convention. But with the exception of DORA above, the introduction of prohibition was delayed until the 1925 Dangerous Drugs Act and by then it was more a question of being a good international citizen than coping with a domestic drug problem. Drug addiction was predominantly an upper- or middle-class problem. Heroin addicts were usually members of the medical profession who had used their own remedies and developed a habit for the drug, or therapeutic addicts, those people who had acquired their addiction as a result of being treated medically with opiates for pain relief (Rolleston Committee, 1926). The seal was set on what was the medicalization of addiction by the 1926 Rolleston Committee, set up to investigate morphine and heroin. Chaired by Sir Humphrey Rolleston, himself a doctor, it recommended that in cases where treatment for the 'disease' of addiction failed, and when the continuation of morphine and heroin would enable the user to lead 'a normal and useful life', they should receive maintenance prescriptions of the drug to which they were addicted (Rolleston, 1926). Drugs were to be a medical matter.

It was not until the 1960s and 1970s that drug use again climbed higher up the political agenda. Drugs became much more accessible and their use was much more widespread. The use of cannabis and LSD was part of a counter-culture that celebrated youth, modern music, sexual freedom and rebellion. The post-war legacy of 'make do and mend' was rejected in favour of the instant gratification offered by drugs. 'Turning on, tuning in and dropping out' (Timothy O'Leary) became the slogan of a generation, and the need to do something about all this became the job of government. In 1971 Richard Nixon declared a war on drugs and the rest of the world fell into line. The 1971 UN Convention on Psychotropic Substances increased the number of the drugs covered by the 1961 Single Convention on Narcotics to include synthetics. In Britain, the key anti-drug legislation, the 1971 Misuse of Drugs Act, came into force. In Britain drugs remained on the medical agenda but the law and order agenda began to take precedence. The enforcement of the new prohibitions became authorities' response to the growing menace of the 'problem drug user' (Lart 1998, 55) and the dope fiend. Drugs, once the province of the doctor and the few, became part of a growing and increasingly worrying subculture. Griffith Edwards points out that 'the new heroin addicts no longer conformed to the profile of the Rolleston era addicts. They were younger and they were into buying and selling heroin' (Edwards, 2004, 116). McAllister notes that 'a more frightening group of users replaces them, primarily younger urban adults, often minorities, who take drugs openly rather than in isolation, and for pleasure rather than pain relief' (McAllister, 2000, 17). Instead of prescribing heroin for heroin addicts, doctors were expected to refer them to Drug Dependency Units where they would be prescribed substitutes such as methadone and forced to undergo a gradual detoxification. A change in the social class and the number of users prompted a different, and much less tolerant, approach to drug use.

By the 1980s this subculture could no longer be managed or contained. Two things happened to intensify the drug problem: the link between the designer drug ecstasy and the new dance and club culture, and an influx of smokeable heroin. Dance music, clubbing and ecstasy helped to 'normalize' drug taking and experimenting with a long and growing list of drugs (Shapiro, 1999). Drugs moved off the campuses. They were no longer a temporary aberration associated with intellectual experiment and student life. Drug use and availability spread to all classes of young people both in and out of work, and this presented the government with the fact that up to 47 per cent of young people (16–24 year olds) admitted they had experimented with drugs (British Crime Survey, 2002–3) and had therefore broken the law. The second change was precipitated in part by the Soviet invasion of Afghanistan. The mujahideen funded their insurgency against the Soviets through a rapid increase in opium cultivation which soon caused a heroin epidemic on British streets. The number of known heroin users, which conceals an unknown number of actual users and addicts thought to be much greater, increased from around 340 in 1955 to 2,700 in 1970 and has subsequently risen to approximately 330,000 in 2010 (British Crime Survey, 2010). Bancroft argues that 'heroin in the UK came to stand for post-industrial decline, rising poverty and disintegration of family life. It enabled members of the ruling elite to condemn not the conditions of the poor's misery but the outlet many chose as relief for that misery, establishing this as a public problem' (Bancroft, 2009, 30). The change in the user groups prompted a shift in the response to drug abuse from policies that were broadly social to those that targeted specific individuals who were increasingly marginalized as deviants. Drugs provided a way of short-circuiting genetic inheritance. Drugs create a false state of being in the user. They enable the user to feel the way they would 'after a successful day's foraging, fornicating or fighting while remaining on [the] sofa watching television, by dint of using heroin to activate [their] forebrain and brain stems systems to give hedonic reward of achieving an optimal state for genetic survival, a drug user can feel and act like Lord of the Jungle while retaining lordship over the remote control' (Bancroft, 2009, 12). This looks dangerously like the start of the heroin republic where the drug users lack the motivation to do anything but find their next fix: a situation that can only be tolerated if the number of addict drones remain very small in proportion to the worker bees.

If the spread of drug use to the lower classes is one danger signal that prompts elites to demand action, another is the association of drug use with race. In Britain the connection between class and drugs has been a significant one. When 'gear' (heroin) goes into the ghetto it is associated with immorality, with economic parasites free-riding and the destruction of family life, authorities are expected to take action to enforce prohibition. When gear comes out of the ghetto and 'infects' the children of the middle classes, as it has done since the 1990s, the clamour for action becomes a demand for treatment for users and punishment for the wicked dealers who wait at the school gate to corrupt the young. In America, the class context has been less evident and instead race has been a dominant social driving force behind prohibition and its enforcement. This is not to claim that race was absent from the British context. Social Darwinism had gained considerable support among some groups and Blackman reminds us that at the end of the nineteenth century and the start of the twentieth, 'a preoccupation with cross-racial sexual relations, xenophobia and fear for the purity of white races was an everyday part of western culture' (Blackman, 2004, 21). Drugs were believed to encourage this cross-racial promiscuity. But it was in America that the problem of drugs and race loomed largest. Drug-using foreigners and minorities would corrupt America's young people. Initially, it was the evil influence of the Chinese and the Negroes that were feared but soon the marijuana using Mexicans were added to the list.

The Chinese immigrants were brought to the American West Coast to build railroads across the continent, but economic depression and unemployment at the turn of the century transformed the Chinese into a threat to American citizens. There were suspicions that the opium habit they had brought with them transformed them into better, stronger workers (see Sandmeyer, 1939). These prejudices eventually led the San Francisco Board of Supervisors to enact the first anti-drug legislation in the form of a 1875 local ordinance aimed at Chinese immigrants who consumed opium. According to Lusane, a far-reaching anti-opium campaign was launched on the basis that 'drugs brought a decline in morals through contamination with "degenerate races"' (Lusane, 1991, 43).

If the western states believed that opium-using Chinese would pollute racial purity, the South feared the 'cocainized' Negro (Musto, 1999, 7). It was believed the use of cocaine would make black men defiant and fearless and the old fear that they would rape white women would be realized. Musto relates anecdotes that told of blacks gaining 'superhuman strength, cunning and efficiency resulting from cocaine' and that 'cocaine made blacks almost unaffected by mere .32 calibre bullets' and this is said to have 'caused Southern police departments to switch to .38 calibre revolvers' (ibid., 7).

In contemporary America this direct link between drugs and race continues to inform policy. It is reflected in the discriminatory nature of crack and cocaine penalties. Federal lawmakers decided that crack was a particularly harmful substance and that this justified harsher penalties for possession. This resulted in the introduction of the 100 to 1 rule. The penalty is ten years for possession of 50 grams of crack but the same penalty applies to 5,000 grams of powdered cocaine. Bullington argues that it was well known at the time that crack was a cheap form of cocaine that was used largely in very poor communities. Since blacks comprise a higher percentage of the poor they are disproportionately affected under this rule: 'In the federal system 92% of crack defendants are black, while only 27% of powered cocaine defendants are black' (Bullington, 1998, 125–6). It should be noted that by 2008 pressure was building up to abolish this kind of discriminatory penalty (Abramsky, 2009; see also 'The Right Sentence', *Washington Post*, 29 October 2009), and that this disparity of sentencing has now been abolished.

Marijuana was thought to be the source of yet further racial and sexual mayhem. It was widely believed that Mexicans were using marijuana to seduce innocent American women. The Hearst newspapers, for example, ran racist drug stories which described how 'evil hemp (marijuana) using, black-eyed senioritas would seduce America's youths into drug use and inter-racial sex (cited in Blackman, 204, 15). This link between racism and drugs continues to the present day. In September 2009, Stephen Gutling, California State Director of the Drug Policy Alliance, a pro-legalization group, wrote an article in the *Los Angeles Times* entitled 'The racism of marijuana prohibition' in which he argues that enforcement of marijuana laws disproportionately affects young African Americans, even though their usage of marijuana is lower than that of whites.' He says 'not surprisingly, given the way that drug laws are traditionally enforced in this country, the burden has fallen disproportionately on people of color, and on young black men in particular'. He points out that in the previous year (2008) 62 per cent of California's marijuana possession arrestees were non-white and that marijuana possession arrests of youth of colour rose from 3,100 in 1990 to about 16,300 in 2008, which is an arrest surge greater than the rate of population growth for that group. The overrepresentation of African Americans is not explained by use rates. According to the federal Substance Abuse and Mental Health Service Administration, the percentage of African Americans and whites who use marijuana over any 30-day period are similar. However, for the 18–25 age group, which constitutes a substantial proportion of marijuana arrests, African Americans regularly use marijuana at rates lower than whites (16.5 per cent and 18.4 per cent respectively), indicating that their overrepresentation may be even greater. He concludes by reflecting that 'in this sense at least, marijuana is a gateway drug, it is a feeder for the criminal justice system, disproportionately for black kids' (Gutling, 2009; see also Dwyer, 2009).

Sociological explanations for prohibition encompass class and race and notions of 'otherness' and they reflect the power of influential groups who have been able to exploit these fears and prejudices to persuade governments to take action. The development of the anti-drugs lobby coincided with a period in history when the spread of democracy encouraged governing elites to be alert to the demands of the electorate. Elite influence remained the key to change but elite groups seeking prohibition were able to mobilize the racist fears and xenophobia of the voters to persuade legislators to ban what we now call drugs.

The key groups that pressed for the prohibition of drugs were the nineteenth-century missionaries to China, the Anti-Saloon League, which extended their interest to other drugs as well as alcohol, and the then professionalizing medical and pharmacy groups. The coincidence of these different forces helped to create a climate of opinion in favour of prohibition.

Nineteenth-century missionaries to China became vocal in favour of prohibiting the recreational use of and trade in opium. It has been noted already that missionaries came home from China with stories of the devastating effects of opium addiction on Chinese families and on Chinese society itself. Their experiences were reinforced after the Spanish–American War of 1898. The outcome of the war was that America acquired the Philippines as a colony. This gained it extensive first-hand experience of the problems of widespread opium addiction in the population.

Other groups emerged to join the missionaries in the call for drug law reform. The first financially viable anti-drug group was the

(Anglo-Oriental) Society for the Suppression of the Opium Trade, formed in 1874 (Blackman, 2004, 10). This group sought to cultivate elite opinion in favour of banning the opium trade. In Britain, the Methodists, Presbyterians and Unitarians all supported the ban, and were strong allies of the movement, seeking to highlight the impact of both drugs and drink on the British working classes.

The medicalization of addiction and the professionalization of pharmacy and medicine played an important part in seeking to regulate, and eventually control access to, drugs. In Britain the 1868 Pharmacy Act, whilst not prohibiting the sale or use of drugs, did require that products containing opiates and cocaine should be clearly labelled and required that anyone claiming to be a pharmacist or chemist had to be registered with the Pharmaceutical Society (Buxton, 2006, 17). Dikötter et al. note that

> the disease model of addiction only appeared in Europe in the 1870s as part of the medical professions' search for moral authority, legal control and statutory power over pharmaceutical substances in their fight against a popular culture of self-medication: where "opium sots" were previously seen to suffer from a moral flaw, "opium addicts" were now increasingly described as hopeless victims in the grip of chemical dependency which only the medical profession was entitled to cure. (Dikötter et al., 2004, 104)

Even after the prohibition of opiates and cocaine in Britain, the medical lobby continued, thanks to the Rolleston Committee's recommendations, to medicalize addiction and to this day the medical profession still sets the agenda covering much of governments' response to drug problems, although it should be noted that they do so in tandem with and sometimes in competition with, the law and order lobby (see Bean and Whynes, 1991).

In America, physicians and pharmacists were also a vocal and effective lobby but less so than their British counterparts. The groups themselves were weaker at that time. The problem facing any lobby in America is that a federal distribution of effort is built into the system. At the turn of the century drug laws remained firmly in the hands of the states (many still do), and the main federal level anti-drug law, the Harrison Act of 1914, had to be introduced through the inland revenue system as a tax law rather than a direct drug-prohibition law.

The prohibition of alcohol had required a constitutional amendment. Americans have a contradictory relationship to prohibition; they seek to champion liberty, but at the same time the legacy of Puritanism demands that it is liberty only to choose the good, liberty, not license. Drugs clearly fall into the latter category.

The sociology of drug prohibition is the story of the success of some groups which have been able to impose their preferred policy on others. The prohibitionists effectively exploited a generalized fear of ordinary people about what a drug 'free-for-all' might be like, fears of the mob or a drug-using underclass, fear of the outsider by making overt links between race and drug use, and a sense of outrage among tax-payers about footing the welfare bill in the modern state. The clamour for drug prohibition gathered momentum when the rise of anti-drug pressure groups, the professionalization of medicine and pharmacy, increased knowledge about the effects of drugs and of the economics of the urban industrialized state, coincided to change the climate of opinion in favour of prohibition. These groups, and the social support they attracted, were effective in influencing politicians to take up the cause of prohibition. The last part of this chapter turns to the political arena to examine further the political explanations for drug prohibition.

Political explanations for prohibition

The 1961 UN Convention makes no specific reference to the political dangers of drugs, but they are there implicitly. Drug use and attempts by authorities to control it can be traced back to the earliest times. In the *Odyssey*, Homer demonstrates that authority's impulse is to be afraid of the corrupting influence of drugs on the people and to try to prevent access to them. The heart of the drug problem is that people want to use them but the undesirable effects of drugs on individuals and society mean that authority feels compelled to prohibit or strictly regulate their use. Authority seeks to control society and drugs threaten to undermine that control. Drug use frequently leads to users losing self-control. Intoxication lowers the inhibitions and users are less inclined, or less able, to obey accepted and acceptable norms of behaviour. From this viewpoint a persuasive case can be made for the total prohibition of all drugs. But such a case takes little account of politics. It is the development of the modern state that helps to explain prohibition, but also why it does not extend to all psychoactive substances.

In Europe we think of the modern state as something that began to develop in the late eighteenth century, coinciding with the bourgeois challenge to absolute monarchy. Owners of new manufacturing and trading wealth were reluctant to hand over taxes for monarchs to squander on foreign adventures and internecine quarrels with their relatives in the ruling houses across Europe. When the American colonists coined their slogan 'No taxation without representation' its sentiments resonated with middle classes everywhere. States underwent a process of centralization and democratization, and their societies urbanized. Divine right monarchy, claiming to rule by the will of God, gradually became constitutional monarchies, or democratic republics, legitimized by the will of the people. The characteristics of the modern states that emerged from this process are not uniform but normally modern states aspire to most of the following: a recognized territory and inhabitants over which they claim sovereignty, states claim a monopoly of the legitimate use of force within their territory; they use armed forces and diplomacy to protect their borders from external attack; they contain a system of police and criminal justice to protect citizens from each other and the state from internal overthrow, and they are administered by a bureaucracy paid for out of taxation. Modern states also claim to be representative, to be based on consent, and to be legitimized by elections and by the provision of public goods and services to their citizens. Of course, not every state in the world has all of these characteristics; some are authoritarian and rely on coercion rather than representation and consent and some are less economically developed and less able to provide welfare for their people. Successful states can impose their rule internally, protect their citizens, exact obedience, deliver economic and other benefits and resist invasion and unwanted intervention from other states.

We have seen how the political sociology of the modern state reveals that certain powerful groups have been effective in creating a climate of opinion in favour of drug prohibition. If moral arguments that drugs are wicked and corrupting were unconvincing, the arguments about the negative economic effects of drugs, the threat of an increasing burden of unproductive addicts, and sociological arguments about neglected children, destruction of the family and society, could still be marshalled. Democracy means that politicians respond to such concerns if they seem sufficiently widely supported by the electorate. Elite groups help to mobilize this support by popularizing their stance against drugs. They are able to mobilize public support in favour of drug control by the use of media campaigns that emphasize worst-case scenarios of drug use and create negative images of drug users, junkies, drug dealers, and dope fiends (see Nutt, 2009). Politicians soon take up the battle-cry of being hard on drugs. When British Prime Minister Gordon Brown assumed office, he quickly announced his intention to reclassify cannabis from a class C back to a class B drug, making clear his intention to be hard on drugs no matter what scientific advisers might recommend.

It is unsurprising that the outlawing of drugs coincided with the processes of industrialization and urbanization. The negative effects of drugs are more significant and visible in the age of the machine, the factory and the working-class ghetto. It is no surprise either, that international drug prohibition coincided with increasing interconnectedness across the globe through travel and trade. Representative governments in the most powerful states recognized that it would be politically unacceptable to ban all psychoactive substances, particularly alcohol and tobacco. Of course, many electors use these drugs and have become accustomed to doing so legally. David Courtwright notes that the liberal treatment of alcohol and tobacco reflected the personal habits of influential leaders and celebrities. 'Personal use of alcohol and tobacco . . . was extremely widespread among western politicians in the first half of the Twentieth Century' and so 'elite conduct therefore reinforced and perpetuated the alcohol/tobacco double standard of most of the Twentieth Century' (Courtwright, 2001, 193). It has already been noted that legal drugs are a source of domestic employment, foreign exchange, considerable wealth and buoyant tax revenues. For authority all drugs are problematical, but it is politically expedient to demonize foreign drugs and shift the blame for drug problems abroad.

Citizens expect the modern state to deliver not only security and internal law and order but also health, welfare and economic benefits. In return, citizens consent to being ruled and paying their tax bill. Drug users who become addicts are a tax liability. More often than not they pay no taxes and are simultaneously a drain on the public purse in the form of welfare benefits and health care provision for what many would regard as self-inflicted wounds. This view is encapsulated headlines such as 'Drug Addict Bill Could Pay for 11,000 Nurses' (*Sun*, 15 November 2010). Politicians have a difficult time convincing the electorate of the need for expensive detox and rehabilitation treatments. Drug prohibition sends a signal from the government to the general public that drug use is unacceptable, disapproved of and illegal. By prohibiting 'dangerous' drugs politicians have responded to calls to 'do something about drugs' and at the same time cleared themselves of accusations of being 'soft on drugs'.

Since the introduction of drug prohibition two trends have exacerbated the problems caused by drugs: globalization has benefited the illegal drug trade and led to increased drug use everywhere, and governments, in seeking to 'do something' about drugs, have created a plethora of self-interested groups which become locked into the anti-drugs policy.

In a bid to increase its democratic legitimacy the modern state has taken responsibility for delivering a range of goods and services to its citizens, but before the state of welfare benefits and economic management developed, the state's main *raison d'être* was its claim to sovereignty within its borders and over its citizens, and to defend its territory and its inhabitants from invasion. Once drugs have been prohibited and identified as a threat to the state's political and social stability, and when the most threatening kinds of drugs are foreign imports, then drugs too become a matter of security and a threat to be countered. Drugs are like an invading army. This explains Richard Nixon's declaration of a 'war on drugs' in 1971 and Ronald Reagan's declaration that drugs are a security threat. Drugs move from the domestic arena of low politics, of health, education, welfare and crime at home, and become the high politics of foreign policy, diplomacy and military strategy.

The drug trade has been able to exploit the incapacity of states to seal their borders in a 'globalized' world, and at the same time the drug trade has reaped considerable benefits from the globalization process. Trends such as increases in business and leisure travel, containerization, deregulation and the telecommunications revolution, have all boosted the global drug trade. Drugs are commodities with a high value to weight ratio, which makes smuggling both easy and profitable (Stares, 1996, 3). The increased use of private cars, boats and planes, and indeed mobile phones, have all facilitated the dealer-to-user network. A local dealer no longer has to risk attracting the attention of the police by having a constant stream of drug users at his door. The use of mobile phones and private transport have enabled dealers to make precise arrangements for the times and venues for covert transactions. Foreign holidays and a global media have increased awareness of drug use and drug fashions. The drug trade is booming and has been since the 1980s, and western European countries in particular have experienced epidemic levels of drug use. The globalization effect has been facilitated and accelerated by the growth of the Internet. Europe, and particularly Britain, is now awash with so-called 'legal highs'. These synthetic drugs are manufactured in laboratories in China and sold globally over the Internet. As soon as one drug, such as methedrone, is identified and banned, a new 'legal' drug appears which may have only minor changes in its chemical composition (European Monitoring Centre for Drugs and Drug Addiction, 2011).

Globalization has been as beneficial for the illegal drug industry as it has been for other industries. Drug producers and traffickers have been able to reap the benefits of economies of scale, and the global media and foreign travel have become advertising agents popularizing a wider variety of drugs to young people across the world. This in turn has increased the pressure on governments to solve the problem – or at least to do something more to curb what to some anti-drugs campaigners is an absolute evil and to others an economic and social burden which may not be evil, but is highly undesirable and a drain on limited resources. So government policy itself also gives rise to more pressure groups which have a vested interest in persuading politicians to endorse and fund their particular 'solutions' to the drug problem. In Britain, over the last thirty years, we have witnessed the development of a whole range of institutions devoted to prohibition at local, national, regional and international levels, whose main *raison d'être* is overseeing, monitoring and reporting on this policy. Looking first at the local level in just one country, Britain, there are Drug Action Teams in every county. These bodies liaise with a whole range of 'service providers' from local doctors to substance misuse nurses, counsellors, child welfare teams, social workers, and enforcement agencies like the police, the courts, the probation service and so on. At national level there is a whole range of government ministries that have a stake in drug policy: the Home Office; the

Department of Justice; Health; Education; Employment and Learning; and the UK Border Agency. Britain is not an isolated example in this regard. Its drug bureaucracy is multiplied many times over in other advanced welfare states and also in less developed countries. There are also burgeoning drug bureaucracies at regional level, including those of the European Union, the Caribbean countries and the Andean countries which co-ordinate prohibition in member states and feed data into a range of UN bodies set up to administer and monitor drug prohibition.

Political explanations for prohibition centre on the responsiveness of politicians in representative states to the demands of interest groups. Drugs are big business, but they are also a significant part of big government. Groups help to create and shape policy but in doing so they breed yet more groups whose bureaucratic survival depends on the perpetuation of that policy.

Conclusion

There is a drug problem because many people want to use drugs and authorities do not want them to do so. Drugs have negative as well as positive effects and it is the former that prompt states to take action against drug use. The resulting attempt at prohibition has ideological, economic, sociological and political explanations. Although these have been examined independently, they are of course connected. Beliefs that drugs are wicked are reinforced by economic, sociological and political reasons for their prohibition. Prohibition has been adopted as a way of fixing some of the collateral damage of drug use. How prohibition is transformed into practical policies, and the success or failure of those policies, forms the subject of the next chapter.

4
How Do States Prohibit Drugs?

States prohibit drugs by passing laws which make the cultivation, manufacture, trafficking, dealing and possession of drugs illegal (in some countries, such as Sweden, drug use itself is also illegal). A change in the law, however, does not necessarily change behaviour. The prohibition of drugs will deter some people who might have considered using drugs, but there is clear evidence all around us that many people are willing to ignore the drugs laws. Ronald Siegal, an American pharmacologist, describes intoxication as the fourth-strongest irrepressible human desire after food, sleep and sex (cit. Reid, 2009a). Law alone seems to be no match for the human drive to use psychoactive substances and prohibition itself may make the forbidden substances even more attractive by increasing the risk and excitement of using them. The law also seems to be no match for those who want to make money from supplying drugs. Prohibition transforms the market for drugs into a black market. This enables suppliers to charge higher prices and make huge profits because of the risk entailed in supplying a forbidden product. Economists in America, for instance, estimate that a quarter of the street price of drugs compensates dealers for the possibility that they might be going to jail, and a third for the risk of physical harm (Islam, 2002).

Prohibition is designed to deter people from using drugs by punishing them if they do. It was noted in the last chapter that prohibition is enforced with the full coercive powers at states' disposal: fines, asset seizure, imprisonment and even capital punishment. Prohibition signals disapproval of drugs and drug use and this quickly transforms itself into social disapproval of drug users. These messages are reinforced by anti-drug stories in the media that highlight the dangers of drug use.

The drug market is international; drugs are a cross-border problem. Until the twentieth century drug control was a matter for individual countries. It was China's inability to enforce an opium ban that demonstrated to other countries, particularly America, that the drug problem was beyond the competence of a single state acting in isolation, and prompted the internationalization of prohibition. States recognize that a change in their own law alone will not be enough to solve the drug problem, so acting alone and together, they try to enforce prohibition with a range of other measures intended to curb the demand for and supply of drugs. What are these measures and how effective are they?

How are market forces used to bring about a drug-free world?

The market for drugs operates like any other market. The price and the quantity traded are the outcome of the forces of supply and demand. If the price falls we should expect an increase in the amount people buy. Those using drugs already may increase their usage, and new users will be attracted into the market. If the price rises the opposite should be the case; users will cut back the quantity they use and those tempted to try drugs will be put off by the higher price. States, therefore, try to intervene in drug markets to drive up prices and choke off demand. To do so they use what are referred to as supply-side policies that seek to reduce the quantity of drugs reaching the market. Supply and demand policies cannot be studied in isolation from one another, since changes on one side of the supply and demand equation would normally trigger responses on the other side. However, in order to make any account of these policies intelligible it is useful to consider each side separately. Internationally, emphasis has been placed on supply-side policies and it is to these that we shall turn first.

Supply-side policies

The Shanghai Commission of 1909 and the Hague Convention of 1912 are important not only because they formalized the international cooperation against drugs, but because they also set a pattern for the future. Thereafter drug control was to be an international matter in which states agreed to prohibit drugs and undertook to enact such agreements into their national law. US leadership of the issue was established and this ensured that its particular list of drugs was the one to be outlawed, and its emphasis on a control and punishment approach dominated. Shanghai and The Hague also established supply-side policies as the preferred mechanism for enforcing prohibition. The belief was that if drugs could be stopped at source then citizens at home would be protected from temptation. This had the added attraction, for the major powers at the time, of shifting the blame onto the outsider. In practical terms, drug crops in the field seemed to present an easier target than the thousands of street-corner deals.

The two key supply-side policies that have been adopted are: crop eradication to stop farmers from cultivating coca and opium, often sweetened with crop substitution and alternative development programmes; and interdiction, a range of measures targeting processing, trafficking and dealing, to prevent the drugs from reaching the consumer.

1   Crop eradication

Crop eradication is a seductive policy and one that is immediately attractive. If all the drug crops could be destroyed at this stage then it seems possible to imagine a drug-free world. When drugs were first identified as an international problem, it was cocaine, heroin and cannabis, the major plant-based drugs, which were thought to cause the greatest trouble and they could not be cultivated everywhere at that time. In essence, the plan could be described as: wipe out the plants and so wipe out the drugs. If only fixing drugs had been that simple.

Eradication can be achieved in three ways: manually, chemically or biologically. Manual eradication involves literally hacking down the coca bushes and poppy plants in the field. But such a method of eradication is deeply resented by the farmers whose most lucrative cash crop is being destroyed. Farmers, often aided and abetted by the drug barons, attack the anti-drug teams sent in to destroy their crops. This invites retaliation and results in widespread abuses of human rights. In Bolivia, the United Movil de Patroullage Rural (UMOPAR), mobile rural anti-drugs units, were notorious for their human rights violations. Similar criticisms have been levelled at the implementation of drug policies in Colombia and Peru (Rojas, 2005). The policy also drives farmers to support insurgents and guerrilla groups who claim to protect them from the anti-drug forces, such as the Sendero Luminoso (Shining Path) in Peru and FARC (Revolutionary Armed Forces of Colombia) in Colombia. Today in Afghanistan, for example, when the Taliban plant mines and destroy the vehicles used for eradication, farmers feel that the Taliban are the only ones on their side (Cavendish, 2006).

Eradication means that farmers lose out on all sides. Their livelihood is destroyed, and they and their families are subjected to violence not only at the hands of anti-drug forces but also at the hands of the drug traders who have often advanced loans to the farmers in anticipation of the crop and then demand a return on their investment. The Ghorian district in Herat province, Afghanistan is about two hours from the Iranian border. Many of its inhabitants are drug dealers, drug addicts or widows. The men folk carry opium over the mountains to Iran where they come under fire from the Iranian border guards. 'Many never return, having been killed in ambushes or executed in Iranian prisons' (*Sunday Times*, 9 May 2004). The women inherit thousands of pounds of opium debt which often has to be paid by giving their daughters to the drug traffickers. Isakhel Surkhrodan, an elderly farmer in Helmand province, voiced similar complaints. He had been forced to give up his seven-year-old granddaughter to an opium trader. He explained that the raw opium the villagers produce is bought by local traders to be refined into heroin. These dealers advance cash to the farmers against the collateral of next year's opium crop. If the farmer is unable to pay his debt, because of the crop eradication programme or even a bad harvest, then the dealers will take his children (Corbin, 2005).

Sometimes farmers are persuaded to undertake 'voluntary' eradication in exchange for cash. This sounds reasonable, but on closer inspection the policy does not work. The level of compensation is often inadequate and in any case it can exacerbate the problem. In Afghanistan the British government offered groups of farmers a one-off compensation payment to destroy their opium crop but this prompted more farmers to plant opium the following year in order to claim the compensation (Corbin, 2005). When the local warlords were paid to carry out the eradication they simply pocketed the money. In Helmand in 2006, farmers were still demanding compensation for crops they had destroyed four years earlier. The British government claims to have handed over £21 million in compensation payments to the transitional authority; however, in 2006 the angry farmers were still brandishing their IOUs for £350 per field, claiming that they had not been paid (Cavendish, 2006).

Manual eradication has resulted in only temporary halts to cultivation. It is slow, laborious and dangerous process for those doing the eradicating and is also very expensive. In Afghanistan after three months' work an American-led eradication force had only destroyed 200 hectares out of 130,000. The eradication force cost $50 million, giving a cost of about a quarter of a million dollars per hectare (Corbin, 2005). The US alone spends $1 billion a year in Afghanistan on a counter-narcotics strategy, which Richard Holbrooke, the US special envoy to the region, described as 'the single most ineffective policy in the history of American foreign policy' (cit. Page, 2009).

Aerial spraying of the crops offers a quicker and, at first sight, a safer alternative to those intent on eradication. In this policy planes fly over targeted fields and spray chemical herbicides. This has been used widely in Colombia, Peru and Bolivia, but again it has several drawbacks. In Colombia, the FARC Marxist guerrilla groups, the drug cartels and the right-wing paramilitaries, the Colombian Self Defence Force (Auto Defensas Unidas de Colombia, AUC), are all involved in the drug industry and are all heavily armed with sophisticated weapons including anti-aircraft guns and ground-to-air missiles, which they use against the crop-spraying aircraft. As a result this form of eradication is almost as hazardous as manually destroying the plants on the ground. Spraying is also a blunt instrument. The Americans insist the spraying is sharply targeted to affect only drug crops and that the chemicals used are harmless to humans and animals. The farmers, aid workers and those monitoring human rights violations are all equally insistent that the sprays destroy surrounding food crops, degrade the soil and lead to a range of symptoms, such as headaches, sickness and rashes, in those people unfortunate enough to breathe in the spray (Hodgson, 2001). Colombia, Peru and Bolivia have become increasingly reluctant to permit America to do this kind of spraying in their countries and in 2007 President Hamid Karzai bluntly refused to allow aerial spraying eradication in Afghanistan.

Biological weapons have been developed which overcome some of the problems associated with both manual and chemical eradication. In the US, Professor David Sands, a leading plant pathologist, has successfully isolated the *fusarium* fungus, nicknamed 'foxy', which attacks and kills only coca plants. In Uzbekistan, in what was formerly a biological warfare plant of the former Soviet Union, Professor Andreas Abdursattar is working on the *pleospora* fungus which only kills opium poppies. Anti-drug warriors see these biological solutions as 'silver bullets'. Such fungi supposedly attack only the target plant and leave surrounding crops and vegetation unharmed. Not only will they kill the drug crops; they will also prevent their re-cultivation in any soil that has been treated with the fungi. Planes attempting to spray the fungi would be less likely to face attack because they could fly higher and the fungi would only need to be applied once to effect permanent crop destruction in those areas that have been treated. The scientists insist that these fungi are harmless to humans, animals and other plants. However, this assertion is unproven, since at the time of writing they have only been tested in laboratory conditions on small areas of the crop. There is no certainty that they could not mutate. Dr Mike Greaves, a British plant biologist involved in the pleospora project, claims it is a 'sensational' answer to the world's heroin problem, but he also admits that he cannot be certain that the fungus is 100 per cent safe (Mangold, 2000). Professor Paul Rogers, a leading British plant pathologist, warns of the wider danger 'once you develop a technology it could easily be misused ... against legitimate food crops' (ibid.). A further problem is that of obtaining permission to use the fungus in those countries where the drugs are cultivated. Unsurprisingly, this has not yet been forthcoming. Recent reports of a 'mysterious' fungus that has attacked the poppy crops in Afghanistan suggest it may have been used there anyway. Poppy farmers in Helmand are convinced that 'they (i.e. American secret agents) have deliberately destroyed the crops by using *fusarium paperavcea*' (Arbabzadah, 2010).

The policy of crop eradication is more complicated than it sounds, but even where it has been implemented successfully, it causes hardship and resentment among those farmers who cultivate coca and opium. In recognition of this, a variety of crop substitution and alternative development projects have been tried. Crop substitution involves persuading farmers to stop planting drug crops and to plant other crops, often with a financial incentive. Alternative development is much the same but entails a more integrated approach including improvements in the infrastructure. Again, at first sight, these seem to offer a solution. The farmers receive compensation for their losses and assistance in switching to new kinds of cultivation. The Laos government, for example, can claim success in getting farmers to switch from growing opium to cultivating asparagus. In the 1990s Laos was the world's third-biggest opium producer. In the follwing decade, in order to secure aid and gain international respectability, it cut production by 80 per cent in the period to 2005 (from 70,000 acres to 16,300 acres). However, even this cannot be regarded as an unqalified success. The Lao People's Democratic Republic is a communist dictatorship and, according to Sebastien Berger, it has 'imposed the reduction with a familiarly strong hand' and 'to prevent growers returning to their old ways one of the government's measure has been relocation, forced or otherwise, of entire villages to lower altitudes, closer to roads' (Berger, 2005).

Afghanistan used to produce grapes for the dried fruit trade and pomegranates for the world market, but the Soviet invasion and the Taliban insurgency destroyed much of the necessary infrastructure and irrigation system. In addition to the patchy poppy eradication programme, there is now a project to revive these traditional crops. But poppy is an almost instant crop. You plant it, you sell it. By contrast, pomegranates require a five-year investment before any return can be realized. Farmers need support during the transition period and infrastructure improvements to the roads, electricity supply and refrigeration facilities for this kind of crop substitution to succeed. They also need security, and protection from the drug traffickers and the Taliban, both of whom want the farmers to continue with their poppy cultivation.

Crop substitution and alternative development suffer from a range of drawbacks. The bulk of anti-drug aid comes from America and US aid is usually weighted in favour of crop eradication, military hardware and the training of anti-drug forces, as well as the capture, and preferably extradition to America for trial and punishment, of drug kingpins. This is not to claim that American money never aids alternative development, but such funding has tended to involve considerably smaller sums and to be for short periods. America's key anti-drug cooperation with Colombia, Plan Colombia in 2000, and, more recently, the 2008 Merida initiative anti-drug strategy with Mexico and Central America, demonstrate that the lion's share of the drug aid is earmarked for gung-ho enforcement. George W. Bush inherited a $1.3 billion aid programme aimed at supporting the Colombian government's fight against drugs. The allocation of this aid was heavily weighted on the military side. Colombia received $860.3 million in military aid, including 20 UH-60 Blackhawk helicopters and 42 UH-IH Huey helicopters, compared with only $68.5 million for funding alternative development. There have been complaints that the US–Mexico Merida initiative suffers from a similar emphasis on military hardware and enforcement at the expense of general aid and development monies. In June 2008 the US Congress agreed to allocate $400 million for the plan, of which $73.5 million is earmarked for judicial reform, institution building, human rights and rule of law issues. However, much of the money will remain in the US and go towards the purchase of aircraft, surveillance software and a variety of goods and services produced by US defence contractors.

Not only do crop substitution and alternative development suffer from lack of funds; they are also often ill-thought out, top-down inappropriate projects which fail to engage the local farmers and local communities (Mansfield and Sage, 1989). New crops call for new expertise and skills, processing plants and marketing, but many drug cultivation areas are in remote areas, they lack proximity to markets, roads are non-existent or seasonally impassable and cultivation takes place on remote, marginal land. In Afghanistan, for example, in some provinces it can take over a week by donkey to get a crop to market. This rules out growing perishables (Jones, cit. Corbin, 2005). An opium farmer from Myanmar provides a clear illustration of why opium remains the favoured crop:

> 'It takes ... one or two days walking up and down the hills and mountains to reach [the] markets ... If a farmer carries only 25 kilo of opium to the market town, he can earn about 1.5 million Kyat (about $1500) for his family. This is enough money for a small family for one year. In contrast, one needs to sell fifteen hundred bags of grain (one bag is 50 kilos) to earn 1.5 million Kyat. It is impossible for anyone to grow such a large amount of grain. And who would like to carry 1500 bags of grain on their shoulder to

sell in town? It takes more than one year for a big family to carry those bags of grain to town'. (cit. Jelsma et al., 2005, 197)

The market carries all before it. There is buoyant demand for drug crops and even though the farmers receive least in the supply chain, the drug crop remains their best cash crop.

Eradication has been tried widely and is unsuccessful. It often exacerbates the problem by stoking up resentment and anti-government feeling. Farmers frequently replant the crops after eradication, even if they have received compensation for their loss. Drug barons secure their raw material by outbidding compensation payments and by intimidation. Farmers sometimes migrate to new, less accessible areas, in order to continue growing the illicit crops and in doing so they and their families experience hardship and environmental damage is inflicted on new areas – for example, the further erosion of the rainforest. This kind of anti-drug policy literally pushes the drugs problem from place to place – eradication and reduction in one area is matched or more than matched by an increase in another. Writing about an upturn in coca production in Peru, Simon Romero comments on the frustration of trying to wage a war on drugs: 'The increase in Peru offers a window onto one of the most vexing aspects of the American-financed war against drugs in Latin America ... when anti-narcotic forces succeed in one place – as they recently have in Colombia which has received more than $5 billion in American aid this decade – cultivation shifts to other corners of the Andes' (Romero, 2010). This pattern is not confined to Latin America. In 2009 the UNODC reported a fall in opium production in Afghanistan, but it also reported that in Myanmar (Burma) the cultivation of opium poppy rose by 10 per cent, and that this marked a third successive year of increase (UNODC, 2009b).

Even if biological weapons were used, eradication will never provide a solution to the drug problem. Supply and demand analysis tells us that, if price rises, demand would normally fall, but it also tells us something about the substitution effect. If the plant-based drugs were all eradicated, drug users and suppliers would switch to other drugs. Alternatives such as methadone and amphetamine-type stimulants are not perfect substitutes for heroin and cocaine, but they are substitutes. Eradication can bring about a temporary blip in the market but little more. When the Taliban succeeded in establishing their rule in all but the northern provinces of Afghanistan, they funded their government largely from a 10 per cent opium tax. This prompted a rapid rise in opium production. In 2000 they did a deal with the international community, so that in exchange for recognition and aid, they would prohibit opium cultivation. They did this with ruthless efficiency so that opium production fell from 4,600 tons in 1999 to 1.85 tons in 2001 (Corbin, 2005). This had little impact on the drug market. Drug users continued to find heroin to buy and there was hardly any change in Britain in the price of £10 for a fifth of a gram wrap, although the quality may have deteriorated temporarily. Before the policy had any impact on the marketplace the Taliban had been driven out of Afghanistan in the wake of America's post-9/11 commitment to oust Al Qaeda from its safe haven in that country. Britain took control of the anti-drug programme in Afghanistan and ruthless eradication was replaced by a more nuanced but less successful crop control programme. This lack of success was exacerbated because the anti-terrorism coalition, dominated by the US, had allied itself with the warlords of the Northern Alliance, who had increased the opium output in their area during the Taliban prohibition. The need to win hearts and minds in the countryside and the need for a western-friendly government in Kabul resulted in the incorporation into government of many of those involved in the opium trade. After the Taliban were driven out, opium production in Afghanistan leapt from 1.85 tons in 2001 to over 3,000 tons in 2002, rising to a record 4,200 tons by 2004 (Corbin, 2005). Eradication is deeply resented and it is usually speedily circumvented.

2 Interdiction

If eradication fails to stop the crop, how effective is the other key supply-side policy, interdiction? Interdiction covers a range of policies that are intended to prevent the crops, once grown, from being processed into drugs and reaching the consumer. Interdiction targets the plant-based drugs such as cocaine, heroin and cannabis at the stages of processing, trafficking and dealing, but in addition the ATSs (synthetics), such as the production and distribution of methamphetamines and ecstasy, and also the interception of precursor chemicals used in the production of both plant-based and synthetic drugs.

Once the drug crops are harvested, opium paste and coca leaves go through several stages of processing in order to transform them into their most profitable forms, heroin and cocaine respectively. Some of these procedures are carried out close to the areas of cultivation. Much of the coca crop, for example, is transformed into coca paste, by adding a concoction of cement, ammonia, lime and sulphuric acid (precursor chemicals) to the leaves, before they are transported to less remote areas where the cartels oversee the transformation of the paste into pure cocaine. Anti-drug forces in the Andes region are not only involved in crop eradication programmes but also smash up the make-shift processing plants to stop the coca being refined at this stage. This kind of activity, like eradication, leads to counter-attacks from the drug cartels and once again it is the villagers and farmers who are caught in the crossfire and lose out on all sides. Interdiction, like eradication, can cause social chaos. Colombia, for example, has one of the world's largest numbers of internally displaced populations with an estimated three million internal refugees having abandoned their homes and flooded into shanty dwellings on the edge of towns that are ill equipped to provide either employment or help for them.

Once the drugs are processed, the next stage is to smuggle the finished product to the market. For South American cocaine traffickers this means smuggling the drugs into America via Central America and currently via Mexico, and trafficking them to Europe via Nigeria, Guinea-Bissau or Spain. It is at this point that the greatest risks are taken by the traffickers and this is where they gain their greatest profits.

Interdiction at the borders has traditionally been the most favoured policy for many countries. It has the advantages of targeting all types of imported drugs and of targeting those who profit most from the illegal trade. Again it aims to intercept drugs before they reach thousands of street-level dealers, the small fry of the drug trafficking world.

However, interdiction is a very costly and complicated process. Taking the US as an example, it soon becomes clear that despite all the ingenuity, hardware and dollars that the US invests in the drug war, it fails to stop the drugs getting onto the streets. The US has over 12,000 miles of coastline, it is one of the greatest trading nations in the world and it welcomes over 50 million tourists a year to its shores. It is impossible to monitor all the official cargo and visitors, let alone those arriving at private airstrips or remote coastal spots. In 1969 Richard Nixon launched 'Operation Intercept' in a bid to curb the influx of marijuana into the US from Mexico. In a plan that Dominic Streatfeild claims was as 'idiotic as it was ambitious' (Streatfeild, 2001, 191), there was extra air and sea surveillance at the border and 2,000 extra customs agents were dispatched with instructions to stop and search every vehicle attempting to cross into the US. In a three-week period, over 5.5 million travellers were searched but not a single sizable marijuana seizure was made. After many complaints from cross-border travellers and a rapid deterioration of US–Mexican relations, the operation was abandoned. 'As an interdiction effort it was a complete failure' (Streatfeild, 2001, 192), and it had the unpredicted consequence of causing a substitution effect among some US drug users, who faced with a shortage of marijuana were prompted to try cocaine.

Operation Intercept failed to interdict any bulk imports of drugs, but that is unsurprising when so many alternative ways of crossing borders exist and when the drugs trade is a highly lucrative and sophisticated one. In 2001 US anti-narcotic agents discovered an intricate network of tunnels connecting the Arizona town of Nogales with its Mexican twin town of Nogales in Sonora province. The tunnels had been dug by the drug traffickers smuggling cocaine, heroin and marijuana across the border from Mexico (Gamina, 2001). Cocaine lends itself to highly diverse forms of smuggling because it can be recovered after being changed into either liquids or solids. US anti-drugs agents have even intercepted dog kennels made from plasticized cocaine (Duke and Gross, 1982, 232). Such innovations are not confined to those smuggling drugs into the US, nor are they confined to the trade in cocaine. Russian authorities have confiscated bags of heroin that have been placed in young onions and cabbages and then the vegetables have grown around them. Not only do the vegetables conceal the drugs, but the strong smell puts sniffer dogs off the scent (Nemtsova, 2010). In 2008 the Dutch authorities seized a shipment of cocaine welded inside metal blocks and hidden in a container of scrap metal destined for Britain (NDS News, 2010). This high-risk, high-reward trade has even prompted traffickers to evade the US Coast Guard by building homemade submarines to smuggle drugs. Between March 2008 and August 2009 the Mexican authorities seized five rocket launchers, 271 grenades, 2,932 assault rifles, a submarine loaded with cocaine and an anti-aircraft gun (Hawley, 2010).

The US and Mexico share a 1,933-mile border. Every day more than a million people and more than 300,000 cars and trucks made the crossing. At one single border crossing, about 15 million freight containers cross every year. Mexico is the third-largest exporter to America, with exports valued at $211 billion, and it is America's second-largest customer, with imports to Mexico valued at $136 billion (Walsh, 2008). Given these figures, it can come as no surprise that interdiction is a failing policy. But it is also one that has sometimes been undermined by other policy goals. In the 1980s Congress refused to continue funding intervention in Nicaragua in support of the right-wing Contras against the left-wing Sandinista. The withdrawal of funding prompted the CIA to make alternative arrangements. It is claimed that that the CIA agreed to a 'drugs-for-arms' arrangement. A blind eye was turned on Colombian cocaine being flown into America if the planes returned via Nicaragua with arms for the Contras (see Cockburn and St Clair, 1998).

Interdiction, like eradication, is often bungled and self-defeating, delivering only temporary reductions in the quantities of drugs reaching the street. In the longer term, the market adjusts and there may actually be an increase in the quantities available. In the 1980s and 1990s, with the cooperation of the governments of Andean countries, America launched 'Air Bridge Denial', a programme of incepting flights thought to be transporting coca leaves from Peru and Bolivia for processing into cocaine in Columbia, the chief exporter of the final product. It was a multi-million-dollar strategy that made use of high-tech surveillance equipment, including radar, satellites and aircraft to monitor the movement of coca and cocaine. The expectation was that prices would be driven up, thereby reducing the levels of drug use in the US. No figures are available for the number of flights attacked or the quantities of drugs interdicted. Some American officials claimed the operation was a success because the price of coca and the amount cultivated in Peru (for the Colombian cartels) dropped dramatically. But by 1996 the DEA admitted that although the air bridge interdiction initiative was considered to be a counter-drug success, it had not caused any measurable shortage of cocaine paste for processing in Colombia (DEA report 1996 cit. Walsh, 2008). The operation prompted innovation by the cartels and increased levels of corruption of officials. Traffickers used fewer flights, re-routing shipments by land and water. They made use of new technologies, including stronger and faster planes and new tactics for evading surveillance. The level of corruption increased as more officials were bribed to help traffickers avoid interception. In addition, anti-American feeling was reinforced because innocent people were killed by mistaken attacks on civilian aircraft (see Weaver, 2010). It also prompted a restructuring of the Andean cocaine trade. Peru and Bolivia began processing more of their own coca and coca paste into cocaine and Colombia became the world's biggest cultivator of coca as well as a processor of cocaine for export. Anti-drug spending increased, but in the end the result was that on the US streets cocaine prices dropped only slightly while its purity held steady (Transnational Institute (TNI), 1999). The TNI report concludes that 'as drug traffickers moved their operations to avoid interdiction and coca growers migrate to evade spraying or other eradication tactics, new regions and actors become involved in drug production and trafficking' (ibid.). Enforcement tends to drive innovation and spread the problem. As new areas become drawn into the drug industry, local production not only supplies the rich export market but also stimulates local demand. Indigenous people experiment with the more refined, and stronger, versions of drugs. The result has been a blurring of the old demarcation between producer and consumer countries. Enforcement has done nothing to curb demand in the rich countries but has spread the problems of addiction in producer countries and with it the negative social consequences of drug use to poorer countries which are much less well placed to fund treatment and medical care.

Interdiction of heroin across the border between Afghanistan and Iran has also failed to stem the tide of drugs, although it has diverted some to the less well-policed republics of the former Soviet Union before it reaches consumers in Europe. New routes mean more countries and individuals get sucked into both the lucrative trade and addiction. West African states have become the latest victims of this process. David Lewis reports that 'West Africans are consuming more of the drugs trafficked between South American and Europe, raising the spectra of rising crime and health problems in already unstable states ... Guinea-Bissau, the landing point for most of the cocaine, saw a string of political assassinations that analysts say are linked to the drug trade' (Lewis, 2010). Afghanistan now has over one million problem drug users. In 2005 the UNODC estimated the number of heroin users in the country to be approximately 50,000. By 2009 this figure was revised to 120,000, a 140 per cent increase in four years (UNODC, 2009a).

Operation Intercept caused a market blip in the flow of marijuana from Mexico to America, but, predictably, shortages of one drug prompted consumers to try alternatives and Americans' love affair with marijuana was widened to include a love affair with cocaine, which some would see as an even more worrying problem. A temporary success in interdiction not only encourages consumers to seek substitutes; it can also encourage traders and cartels to do so. After Afghanistan, Myanmar (Burma) is the world's second-biggest producer of illegal opium. It has a complex history, including decades of inter-ethnic and inter-provincial armed conflict which has been fuelled by opium production. The Shan plateau close to the border with China, Laos and Thailand, the area known as the Golden Triangle, has been a key centre of both conflict and opium production. In 1989 the central government agreed a peace treaty with some of the fighting groups, particularly the Wa State Army, and this in turn has led to a determination to eliminate opium production. The farmers have had their incomes reduced and their lives disrupted; in some areas this has entailed compulsory relocation to the lower-lying land. However, the lucrative trafficking trade has not lost out. The cartels have transferred their activities to the mass production of ATSs, particularly methamphetamine, nicknamed Yaabaa (mad pill) in Thailand, the market for the majority of the drugs exported. The prerequisites for a thriving trade in Yaabaa are precursor chemicals, water, electricity, a willingness to break the law and a ready market, all of which exist in the border area. The farmers have lost their income but the drug trade and the turf war violence continues (Chouvy, 2002).

Eradication programmes attack the livelihood of the least well-off groups in society in some of the poorest countries of the world, including Peru, Bolivia and Afghanistan. In Colombia and Mexico eradication, but more particularly interdiction, have ignited drug-fuelled civil wars in some areas. In all of these countries anti-drug policies have caused civil unrest and undermined the legitimacy of their governments. So why do producer and transit countries cooperate in this process? They could, and do, argue that this is as much a problem of demand that should be tackled in the rich consumer countries, or is at the very least a matter of 'shared responsibility'. Colombia, for example, has adopted a Shared Responsibility stance which aims to get cocaine-producing and -consuming countries to work together to find solutions to the perceived global threat posed by cocaine. Vice President Santos Calderón asserted 'we want European society to understand that it is helping to destroy the Amazon, which it is helping to kill people. Every line of cocaine that a European snorts is soaked in blood' (UNODC, 2010).

Several factors help to explain why these countries cooperate in a process which often causes them domestic problems. They are signatories to the UN anti-drug conventions. Many explanations have been given to account for why states cooperate in these kinds of international regimes (see, for example, Keohane and Nye 1971 for regime theory, and for an analysis applying it to drug prohibition see Bentham, 1998, 119–90). These explanations refer to issues such as identity, states wishing to be seen as good international citizens, the enhancement of powerful elites within a country, bids for regional leadership and so on. There is also the explanation that these countries too are now experiencing the kind of drug use problems that are common in the rich user countries, as traditional practices such as chewing coca are being replaced by injecting cocaine and smoking crack. However, the most compelling practical explanation is money. Most of these countries are dependent on aid from the US and those in Central and South America are also heavily dependent on trade with their rich northern neighbour. The US not only ties these drug-producing and -trafficking countries into anti-drug aid packages like Plan Colombia and the Merida Initiative (Mexico), but it can also, by a process of decertification, withdraw aid from those countries that appear not to be fighting their own corner in the drug war. In 1986 the US Congress passed a bill that requires the president to provide would-be aid recipients annually with a clean bill of health in respect of their anti-drug programmes. Nigeria was decertified in the period 1994–98, Colombia was decertified in 1996–7 and Bolivia has just been decertified (September 2009). Julie Ayling described the certification process as 'a critical part of the coercive strategies used by the US to conscript drug producing and drug transiting states into the War on Drugs' (Ayling, 2005, 376). Decertification involves not only the withdrawal of aid but also the withdrawal of US support for loan applications to the World Bank, which is tantamount to the loan being denied. These countries are poor and often unstable. The writ of the government does not run in all parts of their territory. They lack the tax base to underpin their legitimacy with the kind of welfare provision taken for granted in richer countries. They face challenges from the drug cartels and in some cases guerrilla groups within (for example, in Colombia and Peru) and intervention and threat of withdrawal of aid from without. Little wonder they mostly toe the drug war line even to the extent of letting Americans spray their farmers' fields and extradite and try their drug traffickers in the US.

Despite all the sticks and carrots of the drug war discussed so far drugs continue to be grown, processed and trafficked across borders. If interdiction at the border fails, and it mostly does, then the next line of defence is the police. It is domestic police forces which have the task of trying to stop the drugs reaching the consumer. Their activities include raids on local cannabis farms and amphetamine factories and attempts to pick up intermediate-level and street-level dealers. Having focused mainly on America to illustrate interdiction at the border, Britain will be used to illustrate the problems of policing drugs once they are in the country.

The UNODC has estimated that to influence heroin consumption successfully, enforcement agencies would need to seize about 75 per cent of illegal drugs entering a country. Stuart MacDonald reports that, between 2000 and 2006 the police in Scotland could only claim a one per cent success rate in their attempts to curb the amount of heroin reaching Scottish streets (MacDonald, 2009). While this figure may be seen as shockingly low, the best estimates for drug seizures in most countries are usually placed at around 10 per cent, well below the figure the UN estimated by the UN. A recent (11 February 2010) Greater Manchester Police press release headlined 'GMP Officers in Huge Heroin and Crack Seizure' related how the police, after raiding premises in the Rochdale North neighbourhood, seized five kilos of heroin and crack cocaine with a street value of around £500,000. Unsurprisingly, they hailed the seizure as being 'absolutely fantastic' for both the GMP and the communities it serves: 'This massive seizure of drugs could have caused untold damage on our streets, drug addiction often leads to other crimes such as burglary and robbery, committed by those in need of money to feed their addiction' (www.gmp.police.uk). But that is precisely the point; solving one crime, seizing a hoard of illegal drugs, often precipitates a further round of crime. If this particular seizure temporarily drives up the local price for a wrap of heroin or means that local dealers dilute the quality, then addicts will need either more money to buy the same quantity or a larger quantity to achieve the same fix. If their habit is funded by shoplifting and burglary, then this is likely to result in an increase in crime in the area until local quantities of the heroin and crack are restored. The UK Drug Policy Commission argues that 'Levels of enforcement actively appear to bear no direct relationship to levels of drug use or availability ... enforcement efforts have focused on arrests and seizures, with the aim of reducing supply, but drug markets are large, resilient and quick to adapt' (UKDPC, 2009).

The police are fighting a losing battle against drugs and part of the explanation for this is that drugs are a consensual or victimless crime. This is not to claim that no one suffers because of drug use, but those who do so are only distantly related to the crime. They are in the fallout zone. While the families and friends of drug users may suffer and the community at large may suffer in terms of higher taxes (to pay for the huge burden of drugs on the criminal justice system), higher property insurance, higher prices in shops (to cover shoplifting losses) and increased levels of local violence and degeneration of communal facilities, those directly involved, the user and the dealer, collaborate to commit the crime from which they both benefit. This in turn has a knock-on effect for policing in a liberal democracy since it is assumed that policing in such a society is consensual: In exchange for law and order citizens help the police to carry out their duties. Citizens will report crimes and bear witness in court. But these assumptions are difficult to sustain in relation to drugs. Up to 43 per cent of young people in Britain admit to experimenting with drugs and many of them admit to using them recreationally on a regular basis (British Crime Survey, 2009). This means that even non-users are disinclined to 'grass up' friends who do use drugs. In addition, there is the matter of intimidation. People in some places will be reluctant to help the police, especially if it means bearing public witness in court, out of fear that they or their families may be the victims of some form of retribution. Drug use has also become so common place that it is conceivable that members of the police force have used, do use, or have family and friends who use drugs.

The police experience almost nightly misbehaviour of drunks tipping out of pubs and clubs and may see the cannabis smoker and even the heroin users as a lot less troublesome.

Finally, there is the knotty question of corruption. The British police may seem squeaky clean when compared with those who succumb to the *'plata o plomo'* ('silver or lead' – the bribe or the bullet) in Mexico, for example, but drugs are big business. It is not hard to imagine that some police officers are willing to warn local dealers before an imminent drug raid. In two recent cases a PC Mark Bohannan was prosecuted for conspiring with a drug dealer to provide sensitive police information in exchange for money and for free drugs for his wife, and Michael Daly, a former Metropolitan Police detective, has been jailed for 22 years for his part in a £200 million cocaine-smuggling plot (BBC News, 19 March 2010).

Illegal drugs sustain a huge global industry with a highly efficient international supply chain. People enjoy using drugs and some people have a preference for drugs that have been prohibited. It is hardly surprising that buoyant demand has ensured that supply-side policies are destined to fail. Eradication, by whatever means, causes hardship, resentment and, even when linked to alternative development, is rarely successful. David Whynes tells us that to have any hope of success; supply-side controls need a producer sector with profitable alternative economic opportunities, effective enforcement and to be unable to open up new sources of supply (Whynes, 1991, 475–96). None of these conditions have been met in the drug trade. In a world of global travel and trade and of private yachts and aircraft, let alone tunnels and submersibles, interdiction is doomed to failure. The traffickers factor in a percentage loss of production to cover interdiction losses, trafficking routes and methods are sophisticated and highly flexible and police interdiction, even when it is successful, may only result in solving a tiny part of one crime in exchange for leading to the commission of many more minor crimes. Tackling the serious organized crime associated with the illegal drug trade may simply displace it by leading to an increase in less serious disorganized crime in the homes, shops and neighbourhoods of addicts.

There is, of course, the question of deterrence, the punishment that faces those who are involved in the drug trade. The efficacy of deterrence will be examined after we have looked at demand-side policies, since deterrence is targeted at both users and dealers.

Demand-side policies

Demand-side policies seem to offer little more hope for solving the drug problem than do supply-side policies. We have noted already that supply-side policies are the flipside of demand-side policies. The theory is that if supply is reduced the price of drugs will be driven up and that higher prices will choke off demand. In practice, this has not been the case. Despite all the resources and ingenuity invested in supply-side policies, they rarely have more than a temporary impact on the marketplace. They may trigger short-term substitution effects such as switching from cannabis to cocaine (although they are not close substitutes) as in Operation Intercept, but they seem to have had no measurable long-term effect on drug use. In the case of temporary heroin shortages, price rises caused by shortages may be counter-productive in not only failing to curb demand but actually prompting an increase in acquisitive crime to enable those addicts who fund their drug use by shoplifting and burglary to meet the higher cost of a fix. Economists provide us with an explanation for why supply-side policies that seek to drive up the price of drugs are likely to fail. Drugs are addictive products and thus the demand for them is inelastic. This means that for some less addictive drugs price increases may prompt a reduction in use or substitution, for those drugs that are addictive, particularly heroin and cocaine, including crack, a large rise in price may result in a very small, less than proportionate, fall in demand. It is because governments understand this basic supply and demand theory that they attempt to use demand side policies in addition to supply side. They try, by means of education and interdiction, to prevent people from trying drugs, that is to curtail potential demand, and by the provision of detoxification and rehabilitation, they attempt to treat addiction, and thus cut the demand for the drugs that are regarded as the most problematic. It is to these demand side policies, education and treatment that we now turn.

1   Education

On the face of it, this promises to be an ideal drug policy. If people can be persuaded never to start using drugs, demand would fall, there would be an end to addiction, and the financial rewards of the black market would be eliminated. Organized crime would, of course, continue to exist, but it would drift away from the drug trade. Education takes a variety of forms, including media campaigns, formal education in schools, help lines and literature designed for potential users, users and parents.

Media campaigns have ranged from the widely publicized but seemingly just as widely ignored, US 'Just Say No to Drugs', to the more low-key drugs storylines in 'soaps' depicting drug use as the road to ruin. The then First Lady, Nancy Reagan, played a prominent role in the 'Just Say No' campaign of the 1980s. When she visited a school in Oakland, California a ten-year-old pupil, Angel Wiltz, asked what she should do if someone offered her drugs. Mrs Reagan replied 'Just say no'. Within a year 5,000 'Just Say No' clubs had been formed around the country, but this had little measurable effect on the ever buoyant drug trade. The idea of 'just say no' even crossed the Atlantic but in a less formal, soap opera setting. Zammo, a character in the popular British children's TV drama *Grange Hill* became addicted to drugs. The programme closely followed the increasing difficulties he experienced because of his drug use, which started with glue sniffing and ended up with smoking heroin. More recently (2011) the popular TV soap *EastEnders* depicted one of the key characters, Phil Mitchell, grappling with crack addiction.

Drugs education, of course, is not simply confined to big media campaigns. In Britain and many other countries it now forms a part of the curriculum in all schools, not just secondary schools. The belief is that drugs education should start much earlier if it is to have a significant effect, so nowadays primary school children are also warned about the danger of drugs and how to resist peer pressure. Dealing with peer pressure is important if drugs education is to stand a chance of working. Few individuals go out alone to look for drugs. Initiation into drug use nearly always takes place among friends or gangs, and it is saying 'no' to this kind of pressure that is very difficult for young people who want to be part of the crowd. It is partly to empower young people to resist these kinds of pressure, and to identify for early intervention those who have been tempted to use drugs, that sniffer dogs and drug testing have been introduced in schools. Once again these are American initiatives which governments on this side of the Atlantic have half-heartedly endorsed. In 2004, the then prime minister, Tony Blair, gave his backing to drug tests in schools. Headteachers have been given the power to introduce random drug tests in their schools and they will have the powers to direct for treatment those pupils testing positive, or, in more serious cases, to exclude them from school and possibly to report offenders to the police. Peter Stoker of the National Drug Prevention Alliance welcomed the initiative, arguing that it gives pupils 'an excuse to say no when someone is trying to push them into using' (BBC News, 22 February 2004). Parents can also now buy drug testing kits which enable them to carry out tests on the urine of their children to detect drug use.

However, these kinds of initiative are not cost free. They create an atmosphere of mistrust and may leave young people feeling they have nowhere to turn if they are experiencing difficulties with drugs, Importantly, they may feel that nobody trusts them. Neil McKeganey conducted research into random drug testing for the Joseph Rowntree Foundation and concluded that such programmes 'whilst they might help some pupils, may harm others'. Random drug testing programmes in schools raise ethical concerns about a number of issues: who shoud be tested, consent, confidentiality, how to respond to positive test results. They may prompt pupils to switch from more easily detectable 'soft' drugs to 'harder' drugs. These tests may also undermine the relationship between pupils and teachers (McKeganey, 2005). Positive results to such tests bring a further range of problems. This could result in a child being excluded from school, which may drive them further into a drug-using, and maybe even a drug-dealing, career. In the short term this could be simply a case of finding something to do, but in the longer term it will have an impact on their educational achievement and employability. The International Drug Policy Consortium argue that the evidence base for the effectiveness of drug testing in schools is exceedingly narrow and that 'research so far has not demonstrated that such testing is significantly effective at preventing or reducing drug use' (Hallam, 2010). Drug testing kits for parents raise a further range of difficulties. They convey a clear message of lack of trust. In practical terms, how does a parent persuade a truculent teenager to hand over a urine sample? Testing is unlikely to provide an excuse for a child to say no to his peers. A teenager experiencing peer group pressure to try drugs is hardly likely to admit that their parents test their urine (Millar, 2004).

Media campaigns and formal anti-drug education are supplemented by drugs literature and information websites and help lines, but these too can be counter-productive and problematical. If the literature and the help lines stick to a 'Drugs Are Bad' or 'Just Say No' line, then young people will tend to discount the message. They are likely to know people who have used drugs, enjoyed using them and come to little apparent harm. On the other hand, if these sources provide honest information about drugs they are criticized for teaching young people 'how to use drugs' rather than scaring them into not using them. The British charity Lifeline produces a range of explicit factual advice about drugs. Rejecting the 'Just Say No' approach, it explains clearly the pros as well as the cons of each drug and gives detailed information about safe use and harm reduction. Its guide to cocaine describes it as 'exciting, sexy, enjoyable and slightly dangerous'. It uses bad language, sexual imagery and cartoon strips to get the message across to those who are young, less well educated but likely to be using drugs. This level of realism has attracted much criticism from anti-drug campaigners (Nair, 2003).

In 2003 the British government embraced a new realism in relation to drugs when it invested nearly £7 million on FRANK, a drugs helpline. The name was intended to convey the nature of the information; it was to be frank: accessible, honest and non-judgemental, so that it was likely to gain the trust of young people. It has gained widespread recognition as a source of fairly 'honest' information about drugs. It explains the effects of drugs as well as the dangers. It remains the hope that young people will be deterred from experimenting because of the clearly explained pros and cons. But FRANK has also stirred up controversy, having been blamed for downplaying the dangers of drugs (Henry et al., 2009).

FRANK can also be criticized for being less than entirely frank. In the Autumn of 2009 it sponsored a £1 million anti-cocaine campaign which featured a fictional dog called Pablo, a drug mule who died whilst being used to smuggle cocaine powder. The campaign played on the British love of animals and cocaine and crack users were indirectly implicated in animal cruelty. But the message was an ambiguous one and could equally have been used as a reason for legalizing: cut out the cruelty of the covert drug trade by legalization. A 2010 campaign linking cocaine use to environmental destruction has been equally ambiguous. This has involved much banding about of the statement 'for each gram of cocaine consumed, four square metres of tropical forest is destroyed'. But it does not take much reflection for environmentally conscious cocaine users to work out for themselves that even in the unlikely possibility of this kind of calculation being possible, let alone accurate, this too would not be the case if eradication was not forcing coca farmers to encroach further and further into the rain forest to make a living.

Does drugs education work? This is a difficult question to answer because there is no accurate way to measure the outcomes. Every school may provide drugs education but this may have little or no impact on the levels of drug taking. Research into the impact of drugs education has been undertaken, but the results are inconclusive. The Home Office's United Kingdom Drug Situation Report (2009) claims that 60 per cent of school pupils in England aged between 11 and 15 who were surveyed remembered having received drugs education in the previous 12 months. But this does not tell us if they acted on the anti-drugs advice or ignored it. A BBC report claims that only 23 per cent of pupils who rated their drugs awareness lessons as 'very or quite useful' had not taken drugs, and 60 per cent who regarded their drugs education as 'not at all useful' said they had taken drugs. Even those pupils who claim drugs education persuaded them not to take drugs may never have been tempted to experiment with drugs anyway.

Drugs education and drug awareness campaigns can play a part in providing information about drugs and some of the dangers associated with drug use, but they cannot claim much that is verifiable by way of drug prevention. In 1983 the Los Angeles Police Department launched the highly popular DARE (Drug Abuse Resistance Education) campaign, which combined school lectures, role play, exercises and a graduation ceremony including pledges to resist drugs. It soon became a national phenomenon, and was even taken up by some school areas here in Britain. By 2003 the programme had cost $230 million and involved 50,000 police officers. Despite all this, according to Claire Suddath, this programme produced 'negligible results' (Suddath, 2009). In Nigel Dorn's view, 'no known method of drug education can be said to reduce drug use' (Dorn, 1981). This view is largely borne out by an extensive European-level research project that concluded 'despite some encouraging findings . . . these are not strong enough to alter the view that drug education in secondary schools makes little contribution to the prevention of problems relating to drinking and illegal drug use' (Faggiano et al., 2010).

Research into the effectiveness of anti-drug public service announcements of the 'Just Say No', 'Drugs Mess You Up' campaigns, or the attempt in America to link buying drugs to supporting America's enemies, suggests that they may have 'limited impact on the intention to use illicit drugs or the patterns of illicit drug use among target populations' (Werb et al., 2010a). The 2009 British Crime Survey, which is based on self-reporting of experience of crimes, indicates that approximately 43 per cent of young people (16–24-year-olds) had used drugs. While many young people watched the 'Pablo' adverts either on television or You Tube, this does not seem to translate into saying no to cocaine use, which continues to be the fastest-growing drug trend in Britain over the last five years (Townsend, 2010b). The obstacle facing anti-drugs education is that it has to compete with a modern culture that has helped to 'normalize' drug use. Young people have grown up in a world of drug use. Iconic films such as *Pulp Fiction* and *Trainspotting* centre on drug use. There have been numerous pop songs that have celebrated drugs and their effects, including Bob Dylan's 'Mr Tambourine Man', Lou Reed's 'Perfect Day' and the banned hit of the 1990s 'Ebenezer Goode' with its repetitive chorus line 'eees are good, eees are good'. Friends use drugs, family members use drugs, MPs have used them, sports heroes use them and celebrities use them. Some do indeed suffer ill effects from excessive drug use and publicly check themselves in and out of treatment centres, which they can afford to do. From time to time the finger of blame does point at the rich and famous: 'Celebrity Users Made Cocaine All the Rage Say MPs' was a recent headline in *The Times*, in which celebrities were blamed for being allowed to 'get away' with using cocaine and helping to 'glamorise and now normalize the use of a Class A drug' (Ford, 2010b). The media makes much of the negative side effects of drugs experienced by the likes of Leah Betts, a teenager who died after using an ecstasy tablet and drinking seven pints of water, and Rachel Whittier, whose dead, bruised and crumpled body, with a syringe still sticking out of her arm, was front-page news. But when the pop star Pete Doherty was recently (2009) reprimanded and fined £750 for dropping ten bags of heroin at an earlier court hearing for a drug offence (Shapiro, 2010) this does not send a message of being hard on drugs. The prevailing message seems to be that drugs are worth trying and, unless you are very unlucky, you can get away with it.

2   Treatment

Treatment is the second line of defence in terms of demand-side policies. If eradication and interdiction cannot prevent drugs reaching users and education has only a limited amount of success in preventing people from experimenting with drugs, can we treat drug users to enable them to become drug free?

The word in the corridors of power is that treatment works. The word on the street and from those closely connected to drug addicts is more equivocal. In a pre-election interview in 2005 Tony Blair claimed, 'Treatment is the key to breaking that link [between drugs and crime]. It not only reduces drug misuse and offending, it is cost effective, for every £1 spent on treatment, £3 is saved in criminal justice costs' (cit. Shapiro, 2005). It is difficult to trace the research on which this optimistic prediction is based and was the subject of considerable controversy when Tony Blair quoted the figures. It may have been a popularization of the findings of the 1994 RAND Study 'Controlling Cocaine: Supply Versus Demand Programs'. Based on an extensive economic modelling of comparative costs, this study concluded that treatment is far more effective than either eradication or interdiction in reducing cocaine consumption. It concluded that $34 million invested in treatment would reduce the annual cocaine consumption in America by the same amount as either $366 million invested in interdiction or $783 million invested in eradication. The results of this research, however, may be less relevant to problems associated with heroin use. In order to look more closely at the role of treatment in drug control we will first look at what constitutes treatment, and will then consider the difficulties of evaluating outcomes and end by accounting for the enduring political popularity of treatment as a policy option.

Treatment for drug use and addiction covers a range of interventions from a short spell of substance misuse counselling to helping someone curb their cannabis use, to comprehensive in-patient detoxification and rehabilitation programmes for heroin and cocaine addiction. Under the broad umbrella of treatment there is a division into two main camps: those who are committed to abstinence and those who advocate, or accept, maintenance. The abstinence camp believes that the end of treatment should be that the drug user or addict can live a drug-free life. Treatment should involve detoxification, with or without temporary substitute prescribing to enable the detox to be relatively pain free (in the case of heroin withdrawal) and thus perhaps more likely to succeed. This should be followed by rehabilitation, a period of intensive counselling and group therapy to enable the former user to come to terms with their drug use, and learn to cope with life without turning to drugs each time a problem arises or they experience feelings of loneliness, boredom, or depression. In some cases this kind of rehabilitation can involve expensive residential care for periods varying from four weeks up to a year; in other cases it involves community support from local treatment agencies and voluntary self-help organizations like Narcotics Anonymous.

Those who advocate maintenance argue that whilst abstinence is the best possible outcome, it can be expensive to achieve and is often an unrealistic aim. Most addicts need multiple attempts to get clean from drugs, because, reputedly, addiction is a chronic, relapsing condition. According to the Department of Health, it usually takes between five and seven years for an addict to complete successfully their treatment (cit. Steele, 2007). Addicts often leave treatment early and then revert to drug use. This tendency for addicts to quit treatment rather than drug use causes exasperation to those footing the bill, particularly taxpayers. It raises questions about how many chances the drug users should be given. There is never enough treatment to go round; there are always more seeking treatment than there are funds to pay for it. Beyond the world of drugs prevention and rehabilitation, there are persuasive arguments questioning why limited resources should be squandered on people whose self-indulgence and stupidity have given rise to their self-inflicted 'illness', and, besides, not everyone accepts the definition that drug-addiction *is* an illness.

The maintenance lobby, on the other hand, argues that the key is to engage the addict in treatment by offering prescriptions of heroin substitutes, such as methadone or subutex, and, in a few cases, heroin itself, and possibly providing some counselling, in the hope that this will enable the addict to lead a less chaotic life and eventually reach a stage when they are ready to become drug free. It is hoped that this will be achieved in the community at minimum cost compared with abstinence-based residential treatment. Most of those involved in the maintenance treatment of addicts know that many will continue to use street heroin and eke it out with the prescribed doses of methadone. The demand for illegal drugs is only marginally affected by maintenance treatment in the community. This has led to some experiments in Germany, Australia, Switzerland, and in some areas in Britain, to try what used to be called 'the British system' established by the Rolleston Report of 1926, under which addicts are prescribed heroin maintenance. These experiments claim considerable success in enabling drug addicts to lead what appear to be normal lives, holding down jobs and bringing up their children (see Stimson and Metrebin, 2003). Few would regard maintenance prescribing as an ideal treatment outcome but it does seem to provide a half-way house where addicts can gain some improvements in their lives and in which they may feel less driven by withdrawal symptoms to commit acquisitive crimes for a fix.

In common with most other aspects of the drugs situation it is notoriously difficult to evaluate treatment outcomes. The data available to researchers are less than robust. There is a great lack of transparency and a heavy reliance on self-reporting (Holder, 2009). Treatment providers have a vested interest in the 'treatment works' slogan and this could be a persuasive reason for feeding back only positive results. Addicts who have achieved a drug-free life may jump either way. They may wish to advertise their success and provide feedback to researchers, or they may wish to put as much distance as possible between their new and old lives, and ignore invitations to participate in research. Those for whom treatment has not been a success are likely to be difficult to contact if they have returned to their drug using, chaotic existence. Even those in this category who can be contacted are unlikely to be willing to discuss the extent of their current drug use or their failure. In an excoriating attack on Britain's National Treatment Agency's claim that nearly half of those leaving treatment needed no further treatment and did not return to drug-related offending, Neil McKeganey accuses the NTA of simply analysing client records to see whether those leaving treatment re-contacted treatment agencies in the following four years. If they do not then the NTA concludes they have achieved sustained recovery. McKeganey points out that this same data may suggest that those leaving treatment are too disappointed with their treatment experience to return. He makes the point that evaluating the success or otherwise of treatment must be based on more than analysis of records undertaken by the very agency with a vested interest in promoting the successes of the treatment being provided. He concludes that 'the NTA has done precisely what it should have refrained from doing – claiming near-miraculous success for drug treatment based on the slimmest possible evidence base' (McKeganey, 2010, for a full discussion of treatment see Bean and Nemtze, 2004).

Whether or not treatment works, it has become the favourite option for politicians. In countries like Britain, which have embraced a harm reduction approach to drugs, treatment is an essential component of policy. While harm reduction has played a role in British drug policy since Rolleston succeeded in medicalizing the drug problem, it became eclipsed by the enforcement model when the size of the problem and the type of people using drugs changed from the late 1960s onwards. It was the threat of an AIDS epidemic in the mid-1980s that placed harm reduction back at the top of the agenda. The ACMD (Advisory Council on the Misuse of Drugs), the main source of government expertise and advice on drugs in Britain, argued that 'the spread of HIV is a greater threat to individual and public health than is drug misuse' (Berridge, 1991). The fear was that HIV/AIDS injecting drugs users sharing infected equipment would spread the disease rapidly through both the drug using community and the non-using population. Certainly throughout the world there has been a close correlation between the spread of HIV/AIDS and the spread of injecting drug use (UNAIDS, 2010).

Harm reduction measures seek to reduce the negative impact of drug use on both the user and the wider community. These have included needle exchange programmes to encourage injecting users to use clean equipment, the return of used needles in 'sharps' boxes to pharmacies for safe disposal instead of discarding them in public places where they may injure or infect others, and the removal of the need to share injection equipment with other users. Harm reduction has also condoned the distribution of explicit literature which teaches users how to inject themselves correctly and encourages injecting users to change to safer options, such as smoking heroin or snorting cocaine. Harm reduction has also been a key factor in the growth of the maintenance treatment programme. Those engaged in such treatment are less likely to harm themselves and less likely to harm the community by committing acquisitive crimes.

Treatment does work to some extent, although probably not quite in the way assumed by the public. It certainly cannot provide a quick cheap fix. Tony Blair's endorsement of treatment links it clearly to crime reduction, and it is this aspect of treatment which has made it particularly popular with politicians. People expect politicians to solve problems, but they cannot solve the drug problem. The best that can be achieved is a reduction in the harm it inflicts on the non-using public. Selling the idea of expensive abstinence treatment that takes several attempts before it works, if indeed it works at all, is not likely to be popular with the taxpayer. Why should they foot the bill for self-indulgence and wickedness when there are so many worthwhile alternatives, such as cancer therapies, to be funded? However, if politicians link treatment to a fall in crime, they attract the law and order vote, especially if treatment comes under the criminal justice system in the form of treatment and testing orders, a system under which drug offending addicts are treated in the community and tested for compliance in order to avoid prison, or is delivered in prisons as a form of rehabilitation, or it is comparatively cheap as in the case of substitute prescribing.

Paul Hays, the chief executive of Britain's National Treatment Agency, claims 'anyone who now needs treatment can get it quickly and record numbers of drug users are receiving help ... we have always known that society benefits from effective drug treatment because it cuts crime, improves public health and fosters stable family relationships' (Hays, 2010). He does not comment on the quality or nature of the treatment and he extols the benefits to society but has little to say about the impact on drug use or drug users.

Treatment does work in some ways for some people. It may help to ameliorate some of the worst effects of drugs on society, but it appears to have little impact on either the number of drug users or the demand for drugs. It enables some addicts to kick the habit eventually but some grow out of drug use anyway, and new users come into the market. It is also important to remember that treatment on the public purse is available mainly for 'problem drug users', those who cause society the most difficulties: acquisitive crime, social security benefits and anti-social activities (using and dealing in public places). The Centre for Drug Misuse Research estimates that each problem drug user costs £60,703 a year. By contrast, recreational drug users cost that state only £134 a year (McGinty, 2010). The great majority of drug users who make up 'the demand for drugs' are recreational users who do not come to the notice of the criminal or health authorities. Treatment has no impact at all on this demand.

Deterrence

The supply-side policies of eradication and interdiction and the demand-side policies of prevention and treatment at best seem to inflict only minor dents in the operation of the drug markets. There remains a further policy designed to enforce prohibition: punishment. Fear of punishment is supposed to deter would-be suppliers and users of drugs.

In many countries there is a tendency to decide punishment according to the nature of the drug offence and the type of drug involved. In Britain the key piece of drugs legislation is the 1971 Misuse of Drugs Act, which categorizes drugs according to their perceived harm to drug users and to society. Those in class A, such as heroin, cocaine and crack, are regarded as the most dangerous, and those in classes B, such as cannabis and amphetamines, and C, such as ketamine and rohypnol, are viewed as comparatively less dangerous. Offences relating to supply (manufacturing, trafficking, dealing) of class A drugs attract the stiffest penalties. Trafficking class A drugs can result in life imprisonment, an unlimited fine, or both. Since the 1986 Drug Trafficking Offences Act, and the 2003 Proceeds of Crime Act, such offenders are also likely to have their assets seized. Those prosecuted for possession of drugs also face penalties that depend on the class of the drug. Possession of a class A drug can result in up to seven years in prison or an unlimited fine or both. Thus the 1971 Misuse of Drugs Act reflects an assumption that dealers are wicked and greedy but users are weak, inadequate and naughty.

Long periods in prison and the confiscation of assets are intentionally harsh punishments intended to deter people from supplying drugs. In some countries punishments are even more extreme. We noted already that in Iran and China, for instance, drug traffickers face the death penalty, and in 2010 Gambia introduced harsher penalties against drug crime, including execution for anyone found in possession of more than 250 grams of cocaine or heroin. Presumably, this amount would be considered as possession with intent to supply.

If punishment is to be an effective deterrent there needs to be a reasonable chance of getting caught. Over the past twenty years or so there has certainly been a dramatic increase in the number of people in prison for drug offences around the world. Enforcement of the drug laws has turned prison into a booming industry. The steepest rise has been recorded in America which has been dubbed 'The Great Incarcerator' (Stern, 1998). Imprisonment rates there of 100 per 100,000 of the population remained steady for the first 70 years of the twentieth century, but they have risen since the 1970s, reaching 491 per 100,000 in 2005 (Bewley-Taylor et al., 2009, 2) and this rise has been attributed largely to the drug war policies.

The prison picture is much the same elsewhere. There have also been some high-profile or even spectacular examples of traffickers who have been apprehended. *The New York Times* recently proclaimed 'Mexican Drug Kingpin Sentenced to 25 Years at Secret Hearing' (Mckinley Jr, 2010). It reported the case of Osiel Cardenas Guillen, the head of the notorious Gulf Cartel in Mexico who had been captured and extradited to America, to be tried and, if found guilty, sentenced. In Britain *The Times*, under the heading 'Millionaire Drug Dealer Jailed but Britain's Cocaine Explosion Goes On' (Bannerman and O'Neill, 2010), reported that Craig Rodel, a gangster who led a cartel of 23 gang members involved in shipping cocaine to Britain was jailed for a minimum of eight years. Other members of the gang received jail sentences totalling more than 135 years, and a fellow ring leader, Robert Brook, was also jailed and faces a confiscation of assets order to the value of £42 million. If we look back to the 1980s, when the Cali and Medellin cartels held sway in Colombia, by the 1990s most of their leaders were behind bars or dead, as in the case of the notorious Pablo Escobar.

But does deterrence work? The penalties may be harsh but then so are the rewards from dealing. Even when major cartel bosses are successfully put behind bars there are others ready to take their place. Ted Galen-Carpenter describes this as the Hydra effect: 'cutting off one head of the drug-smuggling Hydra merely results in more heads taking its place' (Galen-Carpenter, 2005). The demise of the Medellin and Cali cartels in Colombia in the 1990s allowed 300 disparate cartels to replace them and make the job of the anti-drug forces even more complicated (Rosenberg, 1996, 37). There are spectacular cases like those above in which so-called kingpins are locked away for years but most of the swelling numbers of people in prison for drug offences

around the world are there for simple possession or small time supply (often to feed their own habit). The Home Office in Britain
estimates that the drug trade is worth £8 billion a year and that it
involves 300 major importers, 3,000 wholesalers and somewhere
in the region of 70,000 street dealers (*Guardian* report, 12 November
2007). Enforcement typically impacts on those who are most exposed
and easily apprehended, the street dealers and the users. They are, of
course, almost infinitely replaceable. Enforcement tends to pick off
only the weak links at the end of the chain, that is, those who actually handle the drugs. Britain spends an estimated £1 billion a year
on attempts to enforce the drug laws, excluding the wider criminal
justice costs, and it is taxpayers who foot this huge bill just to take
users and small dealers off the street. The story in America is much
the same. According to David Sirotu, when faced with criticism about
the cost of prosecuting and incarcerating drug offenders, law enforcement agencies and private prison interests have successfully defended
the idea that it is worth paying any price to jail dealers of hardcore
narcotics. But in 2008 the FBI reported that 82 per cent of drug arrests
were for possession, rather than sales or manufacture, and that almost
half of those were for marijuana, not hard drugs (Sirotu, 2010).

Drugs are a transactional crime, involving illegal trade between
willing participants. The relationship between the level of drug enforcement and reduction of undesirable behaviour is not clear-cut.
Collison explains that if an armed robber is put in jail the average
propensity to commit robbery is at least temporarily reduced in one
particular area. The benefits of arresting a drug dealer are less obvious.
Imprisonment of a dealer just creates an opportunity for a new dealer
to enter the market (cit. Manning, 1980, 252). Manning argues that
drug crime is 'ritualistically enforced with inadequate resources ...
enforcing laws against transactional crime is futile, and enforcement
activities do little but inflate police power, suggesting to an ignorant
public that something is being done ...' (Manning, 1980, 257).

For those involved in the production, trafficking and dealing of
drugs the attractions of big and easy money seem to outweigh the
threat of prison. Prison might pose a threat to recreational users; a
criminal record for a drugs offence may have a long-term impact on
employment prospects. However, most people know that their chances
of being caught are slim and that, in many countries, there has been
an actual (in the cases of Spain, Portugal, Italy, parts of Germany, parts

of Australia and in some countries in South and Central America) or effective (in the Netherlands, and to some extent Britain) decriminalization of possession, so that even if caught they are only likely to face a fine and possibly a caution or referral to treatment. Those addicted to heroin or crack, the so-called problem drug users, have a greater chance of going to prison because they often fund their habit by stealing, dealing or prostitution. But for some of this group prison is a welcome opportunity to try to get clean while having a roof over their heads and regular meals. On 17 December 2010, the *Grantham Journal* reported the case of a mother addicted to crack who pleaded for the magistrates to send her to prison claiming that she could not cope in a community setting and that 'she needs time in prison to get rid of the grip of addiction' (*Grantham Journal*, 2010; see also Bale, 'Drug Addict Asks to Go to Jail', *Evening News*, Norwich, 22 February 2010; and 'Drug Addict Gets Prison Wish', *Brantford Expositor*, 2008).

There may be some truth in the claim of those who say that prohibition would work if it was taken really seriously, but the costs of adequate enforcement are too high, not only in money terms but also in terms of what we regard as acceptable levels of policing in liberal democracies. In China the communists succeeded in curtailing the opium problem. In the 1930s the military assumed responsibility for drug-related matters in the communist-controlled provinces. This entailed 'judicial killing of ordinary people defined as addicts', and in 1936 the National Opium Suppression Commission announced that 'anyone with a narcotic habit could face up to seven years in prison and would be forced to undergo compulsory treatment Second-time offenders could face execution, opium smokers relapsing after treatment would be shot without further ceremony' (Dikötter et al., 2004, 142–3). As a result of these policies many ordinary people were imprisoned and died from epidemics in crowded cells, while those considered to be beyond redemption were simply executed (ibid., 207). Even deterrence this drastic achieved only partial success in containing China's opium problem.

Humans like drugs and they crave intoxication. It is little wonder that prohibition and the panoply of measures used to enforce it seem doomed to fail. However, not only does prohibition fail to solve the drug problem; it also exacerbates it because through causing undesirable side effects. The next chapter will explore these unintended consequences of drug prohibition.

5
What Are the Unintended Consequences of Drug Prohibition?

Drugs have side effects and so do anti-drug policies. People who try drugs may do so for a variety of reasons but an important one is likely to be the expectation of pleasure and altered consciousness. Some side effects may also be a predictable, although not an intended outcome. Users may expect to feel unpleasant withdrawal symptoms as the agreeable effects of the drug wear off. Some effects of drugs may be unintended and unpredicted. In 2006, for example, President Alvaro Uribe Velez of Colombia tried to bring the attention of drug users to one of the unintended consequences of their habit: 'whoever buys a personal dose of an illicit drug ... helps to set off a car bomb in Colombia and to destroy four trees from our Amazon rainforest' (www.Unmultimedia.org/radio/English/print/35892.html). Those in authority adopt drug policies because, for a mixture of ideological, economic, social and political reasons, they want to prevent drug use. They prohibit drugs and employ a range of supply- and demand-side policies to enforce the ban. A combination of reasons explains why these policies have not produced a drug-free world, the basic reason being that many people want to use drugs, they seek intoxication from both legal and illegal psychoactive substances. Drug users would prefer to have only positive outcomes from their drug use. The same can be said of policy makers. They do not want the negative consequences that come with prohibition, for instance the large criminally controlled black market, but they can reasonably predict that a black market is a likely outcome, given that people want drugs and are prepared to pay dearly to obtain them. There are other consequences of prohibition that are not intended and arguably less predictable.

Anti-drug enforcement, for example, has led to the recruitment of younger people, below the age of criminal responsibility, as couriers and foot soldiers in the drug trade. Collison tells us that: 'in some urban areas drug-dealing networks now use very young couriers on mountain bikes to transport drugs, partly to evade police pursuit down alleyways and cul-de-sacs, but also because of the limited punishment available for the young adolescent when caught. The disadvantages of a policy which may encourage younger recruits to enter the drug game and thus be directly exposed to its allure (money, status) should be obvious' (Collison, 1996, 212).

The unintended, even if predictable, consequences of the war on drugs are widely acknowledged. Even at the start of the international movement towards drug prohibition plenty of voices warned that the outcome would be a black market (McAllister, 2000, 42). Britain had already experienced the adverse effects of prohibition, when in the eighteenth century the gin craze led to a ban on gin. This solution to what was soon seen as the drug problem, the excessive use of spirits by the lower classes, turned out to be worse than the problem itself; in the end the government had to replace prohibition with a regime of legalization and regulation. In the Russia of the 1920s the communist regime prohibited alcohol, but the policy was a dismal failure and in David Courtwright's view by the time Leonid Brezhnev was in power 'the Soviet Union effectively became a government of drinkers, by drinkers for drinkers' (Courtwright, 2001, 196). In America by the 1930s, alcohol prohibition, 'the noble experiment', had proved unpopular and unworkable, but not before the less well-off rural population had borne the health risks of bath tub gin, and organized crime had emerged to supply booze to the urban speakeasies. An amendment to the Constitution reversed the prohibition of alcohol but left in place the 1914 Harrison Act, the key federal drug prohibition measure. At the time there was less fuss about the negative outcomes of drug prohibition because drug use remained a marginal activity. It was Richard Nixon's declaration of a war against drugs in the 1970s that signalled drug use had increased so much that it was rapidly becoming part of mainstream youth culture. More drugs were used by more people and the negative effects were being felt by the wider society.

The transformation of international drug prohibition into a drug war meant that the unintended negative outcomes of prohibition itself also became felt much more widely. Even as early as the 1980s some were arguing that the collateral damage of the drug war was more substantial than the intended consequences. Drug use was increasing and the enforcement of prohibition was causing a wide range of negative economic, social and political outcomes. There was an increase in the crime and violence associated with the use and trade in drugs, and negative health outcomes such as overdoses, and the spread of diseases like hepatitis C and HIV, seemed to be exacerbated by prohibition. A growing number of academics, medical authorities and even members of police forces began to raise concerns about these unintended consequences of prohibition. In 1982 Duke and Gross published *America's Longest War*, in which they argued for a rethink of 'our tragic crusade against drugs' (Duke and Gross, 1982). In 1989 Ethan Nadelman, now a renowned anti-prohibition warrior, published an article in which he spelled out all of the negative effects of drug prohibition in the US and argued that these costs outweighed any potential benefits (Nadelman, 1989). Since then, we have heard a large number of pressure groups and lone voices seeking change – either the decriminalization of personal use, or the outright legalization and regulation of all drugs. By 2008 even Antonio Maria Costa, then the Executive Director of the UNODC, the unofficial drug war supremo, acknowledged that the international drug war control system creates some undesirable consequences (Costa, 2008).

The growing clamour for change associated with the critique of drug prohibition will be the subject of chapter 7. The purpose here is to identify the kinds of unintended consequences that underpin the arguments of those wishing to see an end to prohibition, or at least some radical change of direction.

What are these unintended consequences? Some have already been noted in this introduction. It is difficult to arrive at a definitive list or an agreed set of categories. In his 2008 statement, Antonio Maria Costa identified five broad classes of unintended consequences: the creation of a criminal black market; policy displacement from health to enforcement, because the black market and related harms changes societies' responses to drug users; geographical displacement of drug production and trafficking; substance displacement to less controllable drugs; and a change in the way that society responds to users, seeing them as pariahs and subversives (Costa, 2008). On the other hand, as early as 2001 Robert McCoun and Peter Reuter produced a longer and more nuanced list in which they identified sources and bearers of over 50 specific harms associated with contemporary US drug policy (McCoun and Reuter, 2001). Here the list of unintended consequences will again be discussed under the same four headings used in chapter 3 to explain why states prohibit drugs: ideological; economic; social and political.

Unintended ideological consequences

The ideological foundation of drug prohibition is the belief that drugs are wicked. Drugs corrupt the individual soul and destroy society. But western democracies, the countries which have been the driving forces behind international prohibition, are founded on the liberal values of individual rights and free choice. Liberals believe that individuals have rights; states are based on consent and are constituted to protect these rights. America, the drug warrior-in-chief, has even set out these values in its founding document, the Declaration of Independence. This ideology of individual rights has become internationalized into a doctrine of human rights: individuals have human rights irrespective of the country in which they live. The belief that drugs are wicked has been used to justify employing the full coercive powers of states to stop us from using them. This has given rise to what has been described as the paradox of prohibition: the subversion of the values of free choice in democracies to save us from the destruction of drugs.

It is important first to identify some of the things we have come to regard as part of the range of liberties in democratic states in order to understand the ways in which prohibition has eroded our liberties. We expect the law to be knowable, that it will be applied equally, that we will be free from unnecessary searches, that the rules of *habeas corpus* (limits on the time during which the state may detain someone without bringing them before a court of law) will be observed, that we will not be subjected to torture or cruel or unusual punishment, that it is the state's job to prove we have done wrong before it deprives us of our property, our liberty or, in some cases, even our life. We also expect liberal democratic states to operate in societies whose members enjoy the widest possible range of choices, including consumer choices. This list is not comprehensive; its purpose is to illustrate the kinds of things Joe Citizen thinks of as rights.

Problems arise because in many places the belief that drugs are evil translates readily into a belief that drug producers, traffickers, dealers and users are evil. They are an enemy within and therefore their rights are not entitled to the same respect. As in war, the state's enemies have few, if any, rights. Legislators seem to have been less vigilant in their scrutiny over laws that target drugs. The police seem to enforce these laws arbitrarily and the public, egged on by sensationalist anti-drug stories in the media, seem to think the details of drug law enforcement do not matter provided 'druggies' get what they deserve. Barret et al. warn us that the international approach to drug policy relies on 'a moralistic portrayal that demonises and dehumanises people who use drugs as representing a "social evil" menacing the health and values of the public and the state. Portrayed as less than human, people who use drugs are often excluded from the sphere of human rights' (Barret et al., 2009).

The whole area of drug law enforcement raises concerns about the erosion of liberties. Specialist techniques are employed in drug investigations. Surveillance and phone tapping are commonplace; sometimes the police pose as buyers or sellers of drugs in order to trap people they suspect of being involved in the drug trade, and they often rely on rumour and hearsay. Police informers may be of dubious integrity, especially when they provide information in exchange for a reduction in the charges or sentences they face themselves. Jane Goodsir notes that 'the threat posed by drugs has been used to justify a number of measures that infringe individual liberty' (Goodsir, 1993, 144), directly through increased police and judicial power but also indirectly, by permitting our rights to be infringed by a range of other actors including employers, schools, sports bodies who can make negative drug tests a prerequisite for inclusion, and even parents who can now obtain kits to test their children. She goes on to say that 'trafficking ... has enabled politicians to introduce quite intrusive measures directed specifically at drug users and traffickers with relatively little public debate or opposition' (ibid.). This public indifference is explained in part by the fact that drug prohibition is a bipartisan matter. There are individual politicians who are willing to risk advocating legalization or a radical rethink of the drug laws, but as Alex Stevens claims 'politicians usually only suggest decriminalization when they are either on the verge of retirement or at the fringes of power' (Stevens, 2010). Stevens's claim was recently corroborated when Bob Ainsworth, a former Home Office minister for drugs with responsibility for drugs, told Parliament that all drugs should be legalized (although he seemed to mean decriminalized; Ainsworth, 2010). In most countries there is a political consensus among the main parties to steer well clear of what has been dubbed 'the nuclear option' of legalization, and mainstream parties distance themselves from mavericks who think the unthinkable.

In Britain drug legislation has given the police extensive additional powers. The 1971 Misuse of Drugs Act introduced the notorious 'suss' powers: it increased the police's right to stop and search someone on suspicion that they might be committing a drug offence. The 1986 Police and Criminal Evidence Act extended police powers to search individuals, set up road blocks and search vehicles if there has been a pattern of serious crime (including drug crime) in an area. It granted the power to conduct strip searches and intimate body searches of 'those suspected' of drug supply offences. It allowed the police to delay suspects' access to legal advice for up to 36 hours when they were investigating serious offences such as drug trafficking. The 1986 Drug Trafficking Offences Act grants immunity from civil and criminal liability to those disclosing suspicions about the proceeds of drug trafficking. It makes it an offence to tip off someone who is being investigated for drug offences. The police can compel financial institutions to break the customary codes of confidentiality if someone is being investigated for drug trafficking offences. It also reverses the burden of proof. Rather than the state having to prove that a suspect's assets are ill-gotten, the suspect now has to prove such assets were acquired legitimately and are not profits from the drug trade. In 2003 the state's powers in this respect were increased even further when the Proceeds of Crime Act set up an Assets Recovery Agency to investigate and confiscate criminal assets. This enables courts to freeze a suspect's assets at the start of a criminal investigation instead of waiting until they are about to be charged with an offence. Where the court concludes that a convicted defendant has a 'criminal life-style' it will assume that all their assets come from crime.

A recent innovation in Britain's fight against drugs has been the introduction of sniffer dogs to detect drugs on people as they go about their daily business. Sniffer dogs have long been used in prisons to search out would-be drug smugglers among the visitors, but they are now also used in schools and on what Max Daly describes as 'fishing expeditions' when, for example, police and sniffer dogs stand at the entrance to stations, football grounds, outside pubs, at music festivals and many other gatherings at which people are participating in everyday activities, on the off-chance that the dogs will pick out people carrying drugs. Daly cites an example of a mother and her son at a race course who were approached by a policeman with a dog. The dog sat by the boy so he stroked it. The boy was cautioned by the policeman under the suspicion that he was carrying drugs. He was then humiliatingly led off in front of a packed stadium to be searched. Nothing was found. The policeman claimed that the dog never made mistakes and that the boy must have been near drugs or handled a note that had been used to sniff drugs (Daly, 2007). If this policeman's explanation is accepted then we may all be in danger from such searches. Drug use is ubiquitous, so many of us will brush against drugs users from time to time, and it is said that over 90 per cent of bank notes in London have traces of cocaine on them.

The use of drug dogs at all is a grey area. Does such sniffing constitute a search? If it does, then under the 1984 Police and Criminal Evidence Act it requires a 'lawful authority'. Amber Marks, an expert on the use of sniffer dogs, warns that such dogs have been introduced into British policing with little public debate and in the absence of a code of practice (Marks, 2008). She refers to recent research in Australia that found that in three out of every four cases sniffer dogs got it wrong. In the USA, Justice John Souter has stated that 'the infallible dog is a creature of legal fiction' and referred to a body of evidence showing dogs give false negatives between 12 and 60 per cent of the time (cit. Daly, 2007).

The provisions of the various acts noted above and the procedures in relation to sniffer dogs seem to overstep the boundary of what are regarded as traditional liberties with regards to searches, *habeas corpus* and the notion that the burden of proof should fall on the state before we can legitimately be deprived of our property or liberty.

It is also probable that the law is not applied equally. The police have considerable discretion over who to prosecute. Someone who has a wrap of heroin in a small town or village is more likely to be charged with possession than someone with a wrap of heroin in a city. The familiar lament that there is 'one law for the rich and another for the poor' also seems to be borne out in relation to the laws on drugs, and in particular when it comes to the punishment handed out the lawbreakers. It has been noted before that we see celebrities 'getting away with it' and while justice may work, outcomes seem to favour the rich. Journalist Melanie Reid skimmed through a random selection of people who 'in one way or another were found in possession of Class A drugs in recent months' and came up with the following examples: 'Scott McEvoy, 24 from Liverpool – 40 months in jail. Alistair Oliver, 23, from Edinburgh – 29 months, ditto Craig James 23, from Swansea – three years ... James McGlashan, 26, of no fixed address, fined £300. Former Royal Marine, Vincent McGuire, 32, of Gloucestershire – three years in jail ... And Hans Kristian Rausing, 45, and his wife Eva, 44, from Holland Park – a caution and all charges dropped without a court appearance, ... despite being caught in possession of up to £3,000 of cocaine, crack, heroin and cannabis. ... The distinction being that the people in the first section were taken from the massed ranks of the ordinary. The Rausings, on the other hand, are some of the richest people on the planet, heirs to the multi-billion pound Tetra Pak fortune' (Reid, 2008).

The examples of liberties being infringed cited so far in this section are drawn from Britain where the idea of rights and liberties is strong and where rights are grounded in common law, but the same kind of cavalier treatment of rights and liberties occur elsewhere, including America, despite its written Bill of Rights (the first ten amendments to the Constitution). Mike Collison argues that a disturbingly large number of undesirable police practices, unconstitutional searches and seizures, entrapment and surveillance, are now habitually used because of the difficulties that attend the detection of narcotic offences (Collison, 1996, 203). He attributes this to the portrayal of the wheelings and dealings of the drug markets, the violence, intimidation and senseless crimes which accompany the demonic presence of outsiders (yardies, Mafiosi and international criminals), all of which legitimate the doubtful tactics used by the anti-drug police and anti-drug squads (ibid.).

These kinds of questionable police practices in relation to the drug war, urged on by America, have spread to other protagonists. In 2008, Washington encouraged the Mexican legislature to grant the government there new legal tools to prosecute organized crime cases (many of which are drug related), allowing the state to hold suspects for almost three months without charge and to use testimony from confidential informants and government wire taps in court

(Booth, 2010). Clearly, *habeas corpus* can be put aside when it comes to drug traders. Even before this, in 2005, Freeman and Sierra accused America of turning a blind eye or even egging on Mexican forces in the drug war, despite evidence of their widespread abuse of human rights (Freeman and Sierra, 2005).

These are not the only rights and liberties that are being sacrificed in the interests of drug prohibition. In the name of treatment, people in some countries are subjected to what most liberals would call 'cruel and unusual punishments', and, in prosecuting the drug war infringements of human rights in producer and trafficking countries have become the norm. In some countries governments commit flagrant human rights violations against drug users. Drug users are subjected to arbitrary and prolonged detention without judicial oversight. Human Rights Watch, and research bodies such as the Open Society Institute, are compiling a growing body of evidence recording the inhumane and degrading treatment of drug users. The abuse of human rights in relation to drugs has become so commonplace that the International Centre on Human Rights and Drug Policy has been set up to monitor and publicize these abuses in the hope that public awareness will lead to pressure for improvement. Drug users are frequently subjected to so-called treatment for their addiction, but that treatment often has little to do with medicine or counselling and more to do with physical and psychological abuse. In March 2010 *Druglink* reported that Cambodian drug users were being 'tortured' in rehab. It relates how 'a climate of sadistic violence exists in Cambodia's state-run drug rehab centres' (*Druglink*, 2010). Human Rights Watch claims that people in these centres are forcibly detained and are often tortured, including being subjected to rape, electric shocks, beatings, forced labour and military drills'. It goes on to describe the way in which treatment centres in China offer little but compulsory chants such as 'drugs are bad, I am bad', and long hours of forced labour (Human Rights Watch, 2003). A report examining the fate of methamphetamine users in Thailand, Cambodia and Laos in compulsory drug treatment/detention centres usually without medical management of detoxification, describes 'men and women, adolescents and adults, being detained … in dangerous and destructive environments without due process, often without trial and based on arbitrary decisions by untrained officials' (Beyer, 2010). If drug use is treated as a criminal offence it is hardly surprising countries respond with harsh, criminal treatment and that 'anxiety over drug abuse leads many governments to respond with harsh and draconian measures' (ibid.).

Navi Pillay, the UN High Commissioner for Human Rights, raised awareness of this kind of abuse of drug users when she called for a greater focus on human rights and harm reduction: 'drug users suffer discrimination, are forced to accept treatment, marginalized and often harmed by approaches which over-emphasise criminalization and punishment while under-emphasising harm reduction and human rights' (Pillay, 2009).

Violations of the human rights of those 'forced' to undergo drug treatment are not the only human rights violations among the unintended consequences of fighting the evil of drugs. The belief that drugs are wicked has allowed anti-drug forces to get away with human rights abuses in the routine course of their work. There have been many accounts of the physical abuse meted out by such forces in the various anti-drug operations carried out in the Andes. In Bolivia, for example, human rights violations have been constant throughout the period of eradication and interdiction. The Special Anti-Drug Police and Mobile Rural Patrol Units (UMOPAR), an elite force of 58 'leopards' specially trained in America, were notorious for the violence they inflicted on the *cocaleros* and peasants (for a full account, see Farthing, 1997). The current front line in the drug war is Mexico and the Mexican Human Rights Commissioner, Jose Lois Soberanes, reported to the Mexican Congress that his office had collected evidence of widespread torture, rape and murder by police and soldiers in the course of operations against drugs (*Time*, 2010). The Washington Office on Latin America (WOLA), a policy think-tank, published a report analysing human rights violations committed by the security forces against civilians during joint operations in Ciudad Juarez. It described it as 'a glaring example of the damaging consequences of increasing the military's interaction with civilians in the context of counter-drug operations' and concludes that human rights violations are rampant because these soldiers are not punished for the abuses they commit (Meyer et al., 2010).

It has recently been claimed that in Afghanistan the American forces have embarked on a policy of extra-judicial killings, murder by any other name. According to Patrick Gallahue, the US has placed '50 drug traffickers with links to the Taliban on a hit list of people who can "be" killed or captured "at any time"' (Galluhue, 2010). He goes on to report that this gave drug traffickers the same legal status as insurgents and 'blurred the all-important distinction between those who can be legally targeted in armed conflict and those who cannot' (ibid.).

The unintended consequence of the belief that drugs are evil has been a less than scrupulous global attitude to human rights and liberties, an erosion of the values of the societies which prohibition is designed to protect. However, this unintended consequence is even more serious than it might at first appear. A cavalier attitude to the rights of drug users and traders in itself would be sufficient cause for concern, but what we condone in the name of the drugs' evil becomes a kind of canker that gradually infects our other rights. We become less vigilant, police come to hold the law in contempt and our liberties are whittled away.

Unintended economic consequences

The intended economic outcome of prohibition is that the undesirable drug industry will be eliminated – or at the very least severely reduced. There is also an implicit assumption that the costs of waging the drug war will eventually fizzle out when victory is achieved. In fact, the opposite has happened. Milton Friedman described prohibition as 'the drug dealer's best friend'. The drug trade has increased dramatically in the forty years since Richard Nixon declared war on drugs, and the costs of waging the war continue to escalate. The unintended economic consequences of drug prohibition are measured in a thriving illegal economy, which, while bringing some economic benefits to some people and some places, has brought largely bad outcomes, and in the opportunity costs of vast sums of taxpayers' money squandered on fighting drugs which could have been used for health care, education or other common goods.

Steven Wisotsky argues that 'if the cocaine industry commissioned a consultant to design a mechanism to ensure its profitability, it could not have done better than the war on drugs, just enough pressure to inflate prices but not enough to reduce demand' (Wisotsky, 1990). Prohibition has created an economic boom in an untaxed and untaxable industry that is outside state regulation. States which are net exporters of drugs (producer states), such as Peru, Bolivia and

Afghanistan, tend to be aid recipients. They are states which lack the resources to underpin their legitimacy by providing their citizens with health, education and welfare benefits. They often do not even offer much by way of law and order, particularly in the rural areas where the drug crops and makeshift factories are concentrated. Instead of being able to tax their thriving drugs industry, they are under pressure to allocate already scarce resources to drug law enforcement or face 'decertification' by America (see chapter 4 above), leading to a withdrawal of the aid on which they depend.

Of course, the drug industry does boost rural incomes in drug-producing countries. Although the peasant farmer is the lowest earner in the drug chain, the income differential between growing opium instead of wheat has already been noted. However drug incomes remain untaxed at whatever level they are earned and therefore remain beyond the reach of government.

Prohibition means not only that drug-producing countries have to forego tax income; it also brings other negative economic effects. The ill-gotten gains from the drug trade have a damaging effect on other trade and industry. While some domestic benefits may accrue to local tradespeople employed to build sumptuous residences for the drug rich, much of the money is spent either on imports or stashed away in foreign tax havens. Clawson and Lee discuss the displacement effect on the legal economy of the cocaine industry in the Andes and refer to what economists call the 'Dutch disease'. This occurs when a boom in one part of the economy (drugs) causes an inflow of foreign exchange so that dollars become cheap relative to the local currency. Local products then become uncompetitive both on the domestic and export market' (Clawson and Lee III, 1998, 201–2).

Drug prohibition has also placed a hugely profitable global industry in the hands of violent criminals. The levels of crime and violence linked with this trade will be discussed below under the unintended social consequences, but here, from an economic perspective, a further negative impact to consider is that this kind of violence drives out other economically beneficial industries. A liberal attitude to drugs might attract some drug tourists to, say, the Netherlands, but the violence associated with the drug trade in producer and trafficking countries drives out tourists and investment. Johann Hari notes that 'where there is a huge profit to be made in a black market – it's 3,000 per cent on drugs today – people will fight and kill to control it. Arrest a dealer and you simply trigger a new war for his patch, with the rest of us caught in the crossfire' (Hari, 2009). Mexico today provides plenty of evidence to support this claim. the country's unfortunate geographical position between the cocaine-producing capitals of the Andes and the biggest cocaine market in the world in the USA, has placed it on the front line of the drug war. Increased levels of monitoring and interdiction along the traditional trafficking routes across the Caribbean and into the USA via Florida, has resulted in the geographical displacement of smuggling through Mexico. The Mexican city of Juarez, which borders on El Paso, Texas, has suffered extensive drug-related violence, including 2,635 murders in 2008 alone. Jorge Contreras, a local factory owner, laments the effect this has had on local trade: 'a lot of businesses are closing their doors. Our entrepreneurs are leaving for the north (US). Our young are losing their jobs and their only opportunities are crime' (cit. Allen-Mills, 2010a). Few businesses will regard this area as an attractive investment prospect and few tourists from Mexico's rich neighbour regard it as a desirable holiday destination when, as Bronwen Maddox notes, 'killings have spread to the "tourist paradise" of the beaches and north of the border, too, last year. Phoenix Arizona was named the "kidnap capital" of the US' (Maddox, 2010; see also Allen-Mills, 2010b). Even Acapulco, Mexico's premier tourist destination for both domestic and foreign holidaymakers, has become a battleground. Since 2006 nearly 700 people have died in drug-related incidents in the city. Foreign tourists have not been targeted, but Acapulco's reputation has been tarnished. Mr Espejel, a hotelier, complained that in April 2010 2,600 students filled the rooms in his hotel, but in April 2011 there were only 60 bookings (Miglierini, 2011).

The buoyant illegal drug trade, which prohibition has helped to create, has also begun to entice young people, particularly those from deprived backgrounds and localities, into the black economy either as runners for dealers or as dealers in their own right. This is a problem in both producer and consumer countries. There are no barriers to entry, except the law; there is no training, the money is good, the job is exciting, if risky, it is easy to do and it pays well. In times of credit crunch and unemployment it is hardly surprising that, as Alan Travis claims, 'crack dealing linked to gun use is seen by some young people as an attractive career option' (Travis, 2002). Under the headline 'Drug Dealer aged 10 is Arrested', the *Scotsman* recently reported that a primary school boy was among '260 cases of children caught dealing illegal drugs including heroin, cocaine and ecstasy in Scotland in the last five years' (Rose, 2010). It goes on the explain that Strathclyde Police had arrested one youth with 2,000 ecstasy tablets and in another drug bust a child was caught cultivating 350 cannabis plants with an approximate street value of £100,000.

Enforcement of prohibition of plant-based drugs has also had the unintended economic consequence of causing depletion of the natural resources in producer countries. Producing coca for cocaine is an illegal activity and therefore beyond the reach of government regulation. The early stages of processing the leaves from coca into coca paste take place in remote areas and makes use of a variety of chemicals. The toxic waste this produces is then disposed of almost anywhere, poisoning the soil and water sources. In addition to this, enforcement of anti-drug programmes that involve spraying coca plants in countries like Colombia has little effect on reducing the availability of cocaine but it does cause considerable environmental damage (Reuter, 2009a). America claims that the chemicals used are harmless to humans and animals, but this view is not shared by those subjected to the sprays. In addition, the spraying can never be targeted accurately. Much of the coca is planted close to other crops, often on subsistence plots, and the spraying tends to be a rather hit and miss affair. This failure to target the coca crops accurately is aggravated when the planes carrying out the spraying do so under fire from well-armed drug traders. Spraying and enforcement also have a tendency to drive the peasant farmers to migrate to less accessible areas, destroying the rainforest, the soil and the rivers as they go. Colombian Vice President Francisco Santos, in his plea for shared responsibility between producer and consumer countries, described the ecological problem caused by cocaine as a 'silent ecocide' (Santos, 2008). He underscored his point by claiming that the production of one gram of cocaine requires the destruction of four square metres of forest and creates an estimated 625 grams of waste and 200 millilitres of contaminated water which are dumped straight into the environment (ibid.).

On top of all these local economic disadvantages attached to the prohibition of drugs, there is also the huge opportunity cost of fighting the drug war. It is difficult to reach an accurate figure for the global expenditure on the drug war since the monetary costs are measured in different ways and in different currencies. Estimates are also complicated because in some countries spending on drug treatment, which is likely to be incurred even if drugs were legal, may often form part of the costs of punishment, such as Treating and Testing Orders in Britain, and drug treatment available to prison inmates serving sentences for drug and other crimes. In Britain, central and local government spend about £1.2 billion a year trying to tackle the problems of drug use through law enforcement, treatment and education. In addition, it is estimated that between £2 billion and £4 billion of drug-linked spending goes to the criminal justice system, police, courts and probation services (Ford, 2010b). America spends much more. It allocates approximately $9 billion a year to fight drugs, in domestic enforcement, interdiction and enforcement aid to other countries, and this is only federal expenditure (National Drug Control Budget FY2011 Funding Highlights 2010). If state-level spending on enforcement, on police, law courts and prisons is included, then the bill is much higher. Jeffrey Miron, a Harvard economist, found that the federal and state governments spend $44 billion annually enforcing drug prohibition (cit. Kristof, 2009). America is the biggest spender on drug law enforcement but across the globe taxpayers are forking out huge sums of money to fight the war on drugs.

Enforcing drug prohibition is big business. It requires funding intelligence services, police surveillance, interdiction, seizure, prosecution (often with defendants' costs being paid out of the public purse), prisons and probation services. In Britain, for example, it costs around £68,000 to try a drug offender and imprison them for a year. This figure is arrived at by adding the average costs of £37,500 a year to keep someone in prison and approximately £30,500 in court and legal fees. Account then needs to be taken of the cost to society of the former prisoner and drug offender who will have very poor job prospects, especially during a recession, so they will probably have to remain on benefits and return to a life of drug offending. A UK Drug Policy Commission Report points out that most people regard drug users and former drug users as 'dangerous, unpredictable and crucially having only themselves to blame for their predicament (Lloyd, 2010), so it is no surprise that their job prospects are slim when they also have a criminal record.

Some of the unintended economic costs of prohibition were predictable – wars cost money – but what was perhaps much less predictable and certainly unintended was the very steep escalation of both the use and trade in drugs. The unintended consequence of prohibition has been a state of permanent unwinnable global guerrilla warfare in which state anti-drugs agencies and police are pitted against a largely consensual crime which highly inventive and incentivized perpetrators and victims collude to commit.

Unintended social consequences

Some people believe drugs are wicked and that they should therefore be prohibited. It is as simple as that. Part of the wickedness of drugs is based on the belief that drugs make users commit crimes. In 1937 Harry J. Anslinger, head of the Federal Bureau of Narcotics, referred to what he called the 'marihuana menace' when he described the marijuana user as a violent criminal given to rape, homicide and mayhem (Anslinger, 1937). He cited numerous examples to prove his point, including one involving a gang of seven young men who terrorized central Ohio for more than two months and were responsible for 38 'stick-ups' and all boasted they committed these crimes while under the influence of marijuana, and a case in Florida in which a '21 year old boy under the influence of this drug killed his parents and brothers and sisters' (ibid.). Anslinger claimed that the drug caused users to lose all sense of limits and gave them an increased feeling of physical strength. He argued that it caused some users to 'fly into a delirious rage, they are temporarily irresponsible and may commit violent crimes' (ibid.). It was also believed that drugs were hazardous to the user's health and would lead to an early death.

If you ask someone to explain why drugs are banned or why drugs are a problem they will usually cite one or more of the following reasons: they cause crime; people rob you to pay for their drugs; users commit crimes of violence because they are high on drugs; drug users spread diseases like hepatitis C and HIV; drug users cause the degeneration of neighbourhoods; dealers give free drugs to school children to get them hooked on drugs. Of course, some of these beliefs are founded on facts but facts do not give the full picture. It is prohibition rather than the drugs themselves that cause some of these negative social side effects. Drug prohibition not only creates crimes associated directly with the production, trade and possession of drugs, all of which are criminalized in most countries and have contributed to the huge rise in prison populations around the world, but has also contributed to a range of what we generally understand as drug-related crimes: acquisitive crimes committed by addicts to pay for their fix and what are referred to as systemic crimes, associated with the workings of a black market. Drugs can also be harmful to health but again it is drug prohibition that has greatly exacerbated the health hazards and made drug use a much riskier business.

The link between drugs and crime is the most obvious unintended social consequence of drug prohibition. This section will examine this relationship. Afterwards the impact of drug prohibition on health will be discussed.

The link between drugs and crime is incontestable. If drugs are illegal then all users and suppliers are criminals by definition. There is less consensus about the link between drugs and other kinds of crime (see Hammersley, 2008; Mott, 1991). What helps to sustain public support for prohibition is the widely held belief that drugs cause violent crime. Goldstein identifies three types of violent crime associated with illegal drugs: psychopharmacological crime; economic compulsive crime and systemic crime (Goldstein, 1985, 493).

Psychopharmacological crime is crime caused by the effect of the chemicals in the drugs on the user's brain. It is the sort of crime depicted by Harry J. Anslinger in relation to marijuana. It assumes that the ingestion of a drug increases the likelihood of the user committing a crime. Heroin, for example, was believed to destroy the moral reasoning powers so that users undergo a kind of regression to primitive impulses and feel little moral restraint in behaviour towards others (Carnworth and Smith, 2002, 21). There is some evidence to underpin the stereotype of the violent, paranoid crack addict (Honer et al., 1987; Manschreck et al., 1988), but the evidence is far from conclusive. Studies that link violent crime and crack users have 'overwhelmingly focused on the most impoverished and vulnerable sections of society'. Benavie points out that 'none of the gainfully employed crack users who were examined had committed violent acts or other street crimes' (Benavie, 2009, 36). The premise that ingesting drugs cause people to commit crimes or become violent is flimsy and looks even flimsier when compared with the crimes of violence linked to alcohol. Some drug users *are* violent, but their violence may be unrelated to their drug use. Thus headlines such as 'Teenager High on Cannabis Stabs Girlfriend 32 Times' (*Daily Mail*, 18 April 2008) could have read 'Paranoid Schizophrenic, Who Happens to use Cannabis, Stabs Girl', as indeed the small print of the article in this example made clear. Alternatively, drug users' violence may be linked to an inability to obtain a drug such as heroin, which they may be using as a kind of self-medication to calm themselves down. Collins, after analysing an extensive literature on the drugs–violent crime nexus, concludes that 'there is virtually no evidence that pharmacological effects of drugs (alcohol excepted) are major factors accounting for interpersonal violence, when demographic and other correlates of violence are controlled' (Collins, 1990).

There is little doubt that many of those addicted to drugs such as heroin and crack have resorted to dealing, stealing or prostitution to support their habit. This so-called acquisitive or economic compulsive crime accounts in part for the great increase in offences such as shop-lifting, burglary, and vehicle crime that has accompanied the rapid increase in drug use in the last 40 years. In England alone there are approximately 330,000 who are addicted to class A drugs and it is estimated that they commit about £15 billion worth of crime annually (Lloyd, 2009). Extensive research reveals a correlation between drug use and this kind of offence but it does not tell the whole story (see Chaiken and Chaiken, 1990; Mott, 1991; Collison, 1996; Simpson, 2003; Bennett and Holloway, 2007). What research does reveal is that there is a connection between poverty, drug addiction and crime. Clearly those who become addicted to drugs that they can afford to pay for are unlikely to commit economic compulsive crime. The majority of people who use drugs do so recreationally and in these cases their only link with crime is the drug possession itself. It has also been established that some people who already commit crimes may turn to drug use, that in their criminal career predates their drug use. According to Chaiken and Chaiken, however, the levels of criminal activity of this group does increase with their drug use (Chaiken and Chaiken, 1990). The strongest drug–crime link in this category is the acquisitive crimes, which are not inherently violent but may become violent, which are committed by users as a result of the craving for a fix which they cannot afford. In pilot projects, where heroin has been prescribed for such 'problem users', dramatic falls in this kind of crime have been noted (Hallam, 2010b; Shewan and Delgarno, 2005, 33–48). In Britain what has become almost a mass prescribing of methadone, the heroin substitute, to problem users and serial offenders, on the grounds of harm reduction has been accompanied by some reduction in acquisitive crime levels (Hays, 2010; Parker and Kirby, 1996). Methadone may not solve the drug users' addiction problems but it does help to solve some of society's problems with the addict.

So where does prohibition figure in this drugs–crime link? The link between prohibition, black markets and inflated prices has already been established. The difference between the farm gate price and the price on the street can be more than 3,000 per cent. The street price reflects the much higher risks taken by the smuggler and the dealer. The price the drug user pays is infinitely higher than the drugs' costs of production. If drugs were legal, even if tightly regulated, and taxed, they would be more easily affordable, as is the case with alcohol. It is legal risks which keep drug prices high. This is frequently cited by those arguing that drugs should be legalized: it would reduce acquisitive crime. Although this view could equally be used against drug legalization: why add legalized drug problems to legalized alcohol problems? The purpose here is to show that it is prohibition, rather than the simple fact of drug taking, that causes the rise in acquisitive crime that has accompanied the rise in drug use.

Drug prohibition has also contributed to Goldstein's third category of drug crime: systemic crime, which he describes as 'violent and aggressive patterns of interaction within the system of drug distribution and use' (Goldstein, 1985, 498). The drug trade is an illegal system in which the relationships between users and dealers take place outside the law. It is this illegal status of the drug trade that gives rise to the systemic crimes of violence. Disputes arising from an illegal activity cannot be settled by the courts and so very 'rough justice' becomes the norm. There is little evidence to support claims of pharmacological crimes of violence in relation to drugs, aside from the odd exceptional case of aggravated acquisitive crimes where users have threatened or actually used violence, even murder, to acquire money for drugs. The overwhelming evidence of violent drug crime comes from drug markets. If a drug dealer thinks he has been ripped off by a customer, whether it is by a dealer further up or down the chain, or by a user who has not paid a debt, they cannot contact the police or pursue their debt through a small claims court. Instead they resort to intimidation and violence. They may even use such threats to force a debtor to commit economic or violent crimes to redeem the debt.

If dealers or traffickers think that other groups are trying to muscle in on their territory then turf wars erupt and innocent people often get caught in the crossfire. Deals gone wrong, the punishing of informers and competition between rival gangs all cause violence. 'The world of illicit drug dealing is harsh and ruthlessly competitive, with marginal and incompetent dealers often eliminated by rival gangs ...' (UNDCP, 1995). There is plenty of evidence to support this claim. Last year in Rio de Janeiro, on the weekend of 17–18 October, 25 people were killed, including three policemen, ten buses were set on fire and a police helicopter was shot down. The blame for this spectacular outbreak of violence is attributed in large part to the drug gangs who were competing to safeguard their markets and to the police who supply the gangs with guns and who resort to strong-arm tactics and summary justice when dealing with the gangs and favela dwellers in general (*Economist*, 22 October 2009). Mexico provides ample evidence of a similar kind. Overnight between 11 and 12 June 2010 violence between rival drug gangs left 85 people dead in states across Mexico (Lacey, 2010).

These are some of the everyday systemic crimes of an illegal market, but the actual enforcement of prohibition can make matters even worse. Dan Werb et al. found that there is a clear link between increases in drug law enforcement and drug-related violence. They argue that the accepted belief that the enforcement of the drug laws will lead to a reduction in the available drugs, thereby increasing prices and decreasing supply leading to a reduction in systemic violence, is wrong. Enforcement has had little effect on drug availability and use, but it has actually led to more rather than less violence (Werb et al., 2010b). Again, Mexico provides plenty of supporting evidence for these claims. Three years ago, newly elected President Calderón launched a crackdown on the drug cartels. Since that time Mexico has suffered a rising tide of violence in which drug-related deaths have risen from 2,837 in 2007 to 5,045 in 2008, 9,635 in 2009 and figures released on 4 August 2010 put the total number of such killings since 2006 at 28,000 (BBC News, 4 August 2010; see also Bowling, 2010). Many of these killings are indiscriminate. Members of rival drug gangs kill each other but they also kill policemen, soldiers and innocent bystanders.

Prohibition has the unintended social consequence of actually increasing crime levels, making society less secure. But it also has an adverse effect on health, not just on the health of the drug user, but on the health of the wider population.

The link between drug use and health, like that between drugs and crime, is far from clear. It was noted in chapter 3 that drugs can be damaging to users' health. There have been notable cases, such as that of Leah Betts, when drug use has been fatal. There have also been cases where mixing drugs has been fatal for the user, and of people who, after using drugs, have suffered long-term mental heath problems. Syd Barrett, a leading member of the rock group Pink Floyd during the 1960s, suffered many years of mental illness after his excessive use of LSD during that period. There have also been a significant number of people suffering psychotic illnesses linked to cannabis use (see, for instance, Robson, 2005). The problem with this sort of evidence is that it is far from conclusive. Drug use may have caused the immediate health problem but it may have been an effect of an underlying problem from which a person seeks some form of self-medication because they feel anxious, depressed or in some way out of step with the world and themselves (Ramesh, 2010). Besides, things other than drugs can have a dramatic and unpredictable impact on the health of a user, peanuts for instance can be fatal for someone who unknowingly has a nut allergy.

What about the two main class A drugs, heroin and cocaine? Surely they endanger the health of the users and may be fatal? They certainly can if they are used to excess. An excess of heroin can cause a person to stop breathing, and an overdose of cocaine can cause a fatal heart attack. However, over a hundred years ago the Royal Commission on Opium concluded that if used in moderation opium resulted in 'no extended physical or moral degradation' (Royal Commission on Opium 1994–5). During the 1920s an extensive study conducted at the Philadelphia General Hospital found the same to be true of heroin. It concluded that 'morphine addiction is not characterized by physical deterioration or impairment ... When it is considered that these subjects had been addicted for at least 5 years, some for as long as 20 years, these negative observations are highly significant' (Light and Torrance, 1929). In 1995 the World Health Organization conducted the largest study ever undertaken into the effects of coca and cocaine. The findings were that, used in moderation, cocaine has little harmful effect: any problems that are experienced are suffered only by regular high-dosage users

(WHO, 1995). The UNDCP promptly dissociated itself from the report under pressure from America.

It is prohibition itself that dramatically increases the health risks of recreational drug use. Angus McQueen argues that we are burying our heads in the sand if we think that banning drugs 'solves' this problem: 'quite the reverse; driving drugs underground leaves them unregulated and consumers unprotected' (McQueen, 2010). Drug users have no idea of the strength or the purity of the drugs they ingest. It is this that can cause overdoses, or poisoning from adulterating substances. Between April and May 2011, the number of fatal heroin overdoses in Vancouver reached 20, double the figure for April the previous year. This sudden rise is blamed on a batch of double-strength heroin in circulation (*Vancouver Sun*, 2011). In the spring of 2010, for example, there were ten recorded deaths in Scotland of people using anthrax-infected heroin (Carrell, 2010). Drug dealers, seeking to maximize their profits, mix a variety of additives with their drugs in order to bulk them out and make more deals. Some of these additives can be harmless, such as glucose, but they can include materials such as brick dust or sand which, along with poor injecting techniques, can cause major health problems for injecting users. Injecting sites can become infected and ulcerated, and it is not uncommon for injecting drug users eventually to become amputees as a result of inadvertent intra-arterial injection.

The black market cost of drugs and the covert nature of drug use results in people sharing deals and needles. The result has been a considerable rise in the number of HIV/AIDs- and hepatitis C-infected users around the world. The biggest increase in the number of people infected with these diseases, outside of Africa, has been among injecting drug users (see Mathers et al., 2008). Many countries in the West have become more enlightened in this matter and, under the banner of harm reduction, issue free, clean injecting equipment and accurate information about safe injecting techniques. This is not the case, however, in many developing countries which have neither the resources nor, in some cases, the will to adopt these practices.

Prohibition also has a negative impact on the health of those close to drug users. Drugs are illegal and therefore the families of drug users are often reluctant to seek help with their own problems related to the user (Lloyd, 2010). Addicts who become pregnant are also afraid to tell the medical authorities that they use drugs, because they fear that their baby, and any other children, will be taken into care. In America, in some states, this problem is made even worse by threat that drug-addicted pregnant women can be prosecuted for child abuse (see CNN, 23 October 2009; and Jill, 2007). This results in the birth of addicted babies. According to Nina Lakhani, the number of newborns with withdrawal symptoms has risen by 67 per cent in the last ten years. These babies suffer symptoms which include poor sleep, agitation and difficulties in feeding (Lakhani, 2009). Even after the birth of a baby, drug-using mothers are deterred from seeking help in case their baby is taken into care and they may themselves be subject to prosecution. A recent headline on NBC Miami declared 'Drug-addicted Mom Abuses Child by Breastfeeding'. A mother, concerned that her drug addiction might be harmful to the baby she was breastfeeding, contacted the Children and Family Services department for advice. She and her baby both tested positive for traces of cocaine and oxycodone. The mother was charged with child neglect and her baby was placed in care (Fitzgerald, 2010). Drugs are illegal and drug users, and often their families, are stigmatized and marginalized. This can deter them from seeking help when they are ill; their own health is undermined, and in the case of the spread of HIV and hepatitis C, the health of everyone else.

Far from safeguarding the health of the drug users and of society, prohibition has actually increased the dangers of drug use. In addition, it has increased levels of crime, including widespread crimes of violence. These unintended social consequences are seen everywhere and undermine many of the arguments used by prohibitionists to convince politicians and the public that prohibition is the best, and only way, to deal with the bad effects of drug use.

Unintended political consequences

The unintended consequences of drug prohibition examined so far show that it has been costly in terms of our liberty and human rights, in terms of alternative good uses to which drug war money could have been put, and the disadvantages of having an economy skewed by the drug industry. Drugs prohibition has been costly in terms of crime and of health. However, political damage caused by the drug war may be the greatest negative impact of all. Prohibition has transformed the production, trade and use of drugs into an internal enemy of considerable power. The heroin republic may not yet have arrived in the sense of their being a majority of drug users living off the taxes of the few, but it may have arrived in the sense that states have to tolerate external intervention in their affairs and have to accommodate competitors within their territory using state-like violence, providing services, corrupting state institutions and competing for citizens' loyalty. In 1993 Senator Gomez Hurtado, Colombian Ambassador to France, in an address to the European Cities' Drug Policy Forum, told his listeners to 'forget about drug deaths and acquisitive crime, about addiction and AIDS; all this pales into insignificance before the prospect facing liberal democracies of the West ... the income of the drug barons is an annual $254 thousand million ... With this financial power they can suborn all the institutions of the state and, if the state resists, with this fortune they can purchase fire power and out gun it ...' (Hurtado, 1993). His final warning is certainly borne out in Mexico today, where the Gulf Cartel and the Sinaloa Cartel 'after years of mutual beheadings and massacres, the two cartels recently made a truce, deciding the bloodshed was bad for business ... the wrath of both cartels is now turned on the government' (*Economist*, 3 March 2010).

Drug prohibition has handed over enormous wealth not only to drug barons who use it to corrupt states for their own profit, but also to insurgents and terrorists who use drug money to fund their guerrilla campaigns against their own and foreign states. Conflict and drugs have become inextricably linked. Drug production and trafficking funds wars, and areas of conflict attract the drug trade which can exploit ungovernable spaces where law enforcement is weak or non-existent. Gormez Hurtado warns of the threat this poses to 'democracies of the West' but the threat is even greater in weaker and developing states, which are particularly attractive to those pursuing illegal activities (Thoumi, 1992, 37–63). The enforcement of prohibition in such states also helps to spread drug problems to surrounding countries. It was noted above that geographical displacement is one of the five unintended consequences that concerned Antonio Maria Costa when he was Executive Director of UNODC. The illegal drug business reminds us of the domino theory that was once applied to communism. In the Cold War it was believed widely that if one country in the developing world became communist it would have a knock-on effect on the surrounding countries. This has a ring of truth when it is applied to the drug trade. Increased anti-drug enforcement efforts in one country make it more likely that the drug trade with all its attendant ills will spread to less vigilant neighbours.

The unintended political consequences of drug prohibition have helped to undermine some of the key features of the modern state. Modern states claim a monopoly of legitimate use of force within their territory. Armed forces protect them from external attack, police forces and a system of criminal justice uphold law and order protecting them against internal attack and their citizens from one another, they are administered by a bureaucracy, paid for out of taxation, and the provision of goods and services helps them to arouse loyalty and consent from their citizens. A state 'cannot have rivals within its own territories as a law-making power and an object of allegiance' (Skinner, 1978). A state recognizes no rival claims within its borders or rule of external powers. Drug prohibition has led to widespread corruption of the institutions of states. Police, criminal justice systems, armies, bureaucracies and politicians are never immune to the attractions of money. Drug money has enabled drug cartels and insurgent groups to fund private armies which compete with the state to provide law and order, and drug money also fuels civil and inter-cartel wars. States cannot tax this hugely lucrative illegal industry. This has allowed drug lords and guerrilla groups to legitimate their own activities by providing the kinds of services that states in other countries provide to win the hearts and minds of citizens. In addition to all these internal threats to a state's sovereignty to rule its own territory, there are also the external threats in the form of coercive intervention from countries such as America dedicated to rooting out the drug evil and willing to use aid as a weapon in the fight.

Colombia has become synonymous with the negative side of both the drug trade and of drug prohibition. Its sovereignty is challenged from within by guerrilla groups and drug cartels and from outside by American intervention in pursuit of a victory against drugs. There are other reasons for American intervention in Colombia such as ensuring that left-wing guerrillas are kept down and protecting the valuable investments of American citizens in the country, but drugs do provide a 'catch-all' rationale to sell interventionist policies to taxpayers at home (Blackman, 2004). Drugs are not the only cause of Colombia's difficulties, but they have provided the money that has enabled other Colombian groups to wage conflicts both against each other and against the state.

In the mid-1970s the commencement of American's love affair with cocaine coincided with the increased willingness in parts of Colombia to turn to the illicit economy. By the end of the decade Colombia dominated the cocaine trade and the Medellin cartel, directed by the infamous Pablo Escobar, and the Cali cartel, dominated the manufacture and trafficking of cocaine inside Colombia.

Some of Colombia's problems predate its pre-eminence in the drug trade. Much of Colombia's wealth is linked with land which is owned and controlled by 0.4 per cent of the population. One-quarter of the population live below the $2-a-day poverty line, lacking access to mains water, electricity, proper housing, education and medical care, and living in areas which remain beyond the reach of the state. In these areas the presence of the state in terms of providing services or even basic law and order is virtually unknown. It is also a country in which the resort to violence to settle disputes between individuals and even competing political parties has become a familiar part of life. This even gave rise to the years 1948–58 becoming dubbed *La Violencia* because of the constant resort to violence in the state and society.

Given the huge disparities in wealth and power in Colombia, it is hardly surprising that it proved to be fertile ground for left-wing guerrilla groups seeking to overthrow the state and redistribute land. Since the early 1960s, and more or less ever since, Colombia has been waging a war against left-wing guerrillas, particularly the Marxist FARC (Revolutionary Armed Forces of Colombia) and, to a lesser extent, the ELN (National Liberation Front). By the 1980s the drug cartels and the right-wing paramilitary group the AUC (Colombian Self-Defence Army) had joined the fight. The AUC inhabits a sort of *demi-monde*, part private army of the drug barons, part vigilante force for the landowners seeking protection against FARC, and partly composed of and condoned by the state institutions of the army and the police (see Crandall, 2008, for an account of the 'parapolitics' scandal). Not only are these groups fighting each other. They are also fighting the state, albeit for different reasons. The narcos fight to protect their profits from the anti-drug forces, the left-wing guerrillas fight for the revolution, but they are all funded by the illegal drug trade. Drug money buys soldiers and highly sophisticated weapons, but it also provides the wherewithal for these groups to compete with the state for the hearts and minds of the citizens. Pablo Escobar was regarded by many in the Medellin area as a kind of Robin Hood. He was violent, licentious and self-indulgent. He built himself luxury houses, owned planes, a private zoo and lived a playboy lifestyle, but he also built houses, schools and sports centres for the poor of Medellin. The FARC also provide law and order and services in the areas they control. They police the streets, settle disputes and provide help to the poor. In the 1980s the drug cartels, and today the FARC, have been able to create a state within a state.

Drug money has undermined Colombian state institutions; it has been used to corrupt parts of the army, the police, the judiciary and the politicians. Faced with the choice of *plata o plomo* (the silver or the lead (bullet)), most choose the silver. In any case, some Colombians doubt the wisdom of the war against drugs. It is a lucrative industry that provides much-needed jobs. It is seen more as a problem of demand, rather than supply. It brings in wealth and services, so why should Colombia worry about America's drug problem?

Guerrilla groups and narcos alike benefit from drugs. Despite the Marxist qualms about drugs, they tax them, cultivate them and now-adays also traffic drugs (Felbab-Brown, 2009, 81–2). The narcos are in it for the profits in any case. The Colombian state cannot rely on its functionaries and institutions; it cannot tax one of its most lucrative products to enable it to legitimate itself by providing services for its citizens. On top of all these difficulties it has American interven-tion to contend with. Americans demand that it extradite Colombian citizens to America to be tried for drug trafficking offences, beyond Colombia's own corruptible and corrupted police and courts. According to Russell Crandall, by mid-2007 the Uribe administration had extradited more than 500 Colombians to the USA on drugs-related charges (Crandall, 2008, 170). America sends groups of armed anti-drugs teams to train and 'help' Colombian anti-drugs efforts and coerces invitations for the likes of Dyncorp to spray chemicals on Colombian fields. The Colombian government tried to do some-thing about a whole range of these difficulties in President Pastrana's initiative, Plan Colombia, which included projects to address some of the underlying problems of poverty and peace settlements with the guerrillas. The focus of the plan was on achieving peace and ending violence. America agreed to help fund the plan but only after redrafting it, so that some of the original peace initiative intentions became secondary to the anti-drug programme emphasizing enforcement (Livingstone, 2003).

Colombia is the paradigm but not the only case of the way in which the unintended political consequence of drug prohibition have served to exacerbate local conflict and weaken already politically unstable states. Afghanistan provides another spectacular example of the complex mix of illegal drugs, insurgency, ethnic conflict and international intervention. Foreign forces seek to prop up a weak unpopular regime and wage a simultaneous and mutually incompatible war on drugs and war on terror (see Felbab-Brown, 2009). In 2001, after the 9/11 attack on the Twin Towers, America, aided and abetted by Britain and a smallish coalition of other countries, invaded Afghanistan to drive out the Taliban government, which sheltered and sympathized with Al Qaeda. It had temporary success against the Taliban and set up a pro-western regime based on the Northern Alliance, a group of war lords who had resisted the Taliban takeover. Attention was then deflected towards Iraq. The opium crop in Afghanistan suddenly expanded from virtually nothing in the final years of the Taliban rule to a record 4,200 tons by 2004, enabling Afghanistan to become the supplier of 90 per cent of the world's illegal opium for the heroin trade. When the conflict in Iraq began to settle down, the attention of America and its allies again began to refocus on Afghanistan which by 2007 was suffering from renewed violence, rampant drug production and the reappearance of the Taliban. Attempts to curb opium cultivation, that is, to enforce drug prohibition, exacerbated all these tensions and increased the levels of violence. The Taliban have been able to use intimidation and to exploit anti-American sentiment, aroused partly by crop eradication policies, to win the hearts and minds of the peasants and drug gangs. Taxing drug production provides the Taliban with the resources to fight the western (NATO) forces occupying Afghanistan. Any attempt to enforce the opium ban coverts peasant farmers into Taliban sympathizers. Alexander McQueen, reflecting on the situation in Afghanistan, noted that 'the West finances both sides of the conflict. On the one side, soldiers die and our tax money is spent to uphold a government riddled with drug-related corruption. On the other, the huge profits from an illegal heroin trade supply over 60 per cent of the Taliban's finance' (McQueen, 2010).

The enforcement of prohibition in one country also has the effect of shifting the political and economic problems of drug production on to other countries. The main trafficking route for Afghan opium was via Pakistan and Iran. A decade of counter-narcotic enforcement and interdiction of traffickers by Iran has caused geographical displacement with new smuggling routes now opening up through the Russian Federation and Eastern Europe. Domestic drug mafias have sprung up in Kazakhstan, Kyrgyzstan, Tajikistan, Turkmenistan and Uzbekistan, and new routes bring with them new kinds of drug use problems, and the systemic violence and corruption along with them (Makarenko, 2002).

Mexico has become the latest state to suffer from the collateral damage of the enforcement of drug prohibition. Although a source of marijuana for the USA, before the 1990s Mexico had little involvement in the cocaine trade. The preferred route of smugglers was from Colombia via the Caribbean, particularly Jamaica and the Dominican Republic, thence via Florida into the huge US market. But some success with interdiction along this route shifted trafficking to Mexico. This, combined with President Calderón's determination to fight the drug war, has brought much of Mexico to the verge of civil war, with drug cartels fighting each other and also taking on the Mexican Army. The president has been forced to deploy the army because most of the state and federal police are in the pay of the drug cartels or have been intimidated to ensure their collusion or silence. Even the army, or parts of it, has succumbed to corruption. In the 1990s, one entire unit of the army Special Forces deserted to form a paramilitary group called the Zetas, who work as enforcers to help the Gulf Cartel in its bid to take over the turf of rival cartels. President Calderón's commitment to drug law enforcement is not endorsed by all of his countrymen. According to William Booth, 'One by one, the government of President Filipe Calderón has quietly released drugs implicated politicians as federal prosecutors dropped their cases and judges ordered them set free for lack of evidence' (Booth, 2010). Mexico is clearly in the grip not only of drug trafficking, but of all of the violence and corruption of political institutions that accompanies any attempt to enforce prohibition. Mexico's problems are also beginning to trouble its neighbours; Guatemala, El Salvador and Honduras are also plagued by drug-related violence, conforming to what is becoming a pattern of one drug state 'infecting' adversely those around it.

A new front line in the drug war is already opening up in Africa. As far back as 1996, Nigeria was decertified by America for failing to take sufficiently rigorous action against South American drug traffickers who were beginning to use it as a stepping stone to the European drug market. Market saturation in America has prompted the cocaine cartels to look to expanding their business in Europe and Asia where there is rising demand for cocaine. Interpol has warned that Mozambique is increasingly becoming a hub for trafficking drugs from Latin America to Europe (BBC News, 14 July 2010). Misha Glenny notes that West Africa is slipping slowly towards ungovernability. Burkina Faso has tried to get the UN Security Council to address Africa's new war, the drug war. Glenny describes the way in which over the past five years that the coastal countries of West Africa have fallen like dominoes to an assault launched from distant Colombia, Venezuela and Mexico as some of the world's most ruthless drug cartels seek to bring these territories under their control (Glenny, 2009). Cape Verde, Sierra Leone, Liberia, Guinea, Nigeria, Senegal, the Ivory Coast and Togo are all major ports of entry for the cocaine (Glenny, 2009). Where the drugs traffic goes, corruption and violence go also, and attempts at enforcement of prohibition escalate all these problems.

The political collateral damage from drug prohibition further weakens and destabilizes already weak, impoverished 'failing' states. Enforcement ensures that the problem will migrate to neighbouring states or even to countries in a distant continent. Instead of saving countries from the evil of drugs, drug prohibition brings state destruction from the corruption and violence associated with black markets and enforcement.

The intention of prohibition is to save societies and individuals from the harms of drug use. Despite this, the supply and demand for drugs continues to increase. International prohibition began in 1909. In 1971 Richard Nixon declared a war on drugs. In 1982 Ronald Reagan securitized the drug problem, transforming it from a matter of criminality to a matter of national security that required the engagement not just of police and customs, but also of armies and security agencies. The UN General Assembly declared the 1990s to be a decade against drugs; it might as well have declared a decade for drugs because drug use and supply increased dramatically throughout this period. Prohibition has been the pavement of good intention on the road to hell. As Peter Reuter argues: 'It is reasonable to conclude that international drug control efforts can do more to affect where drugs are produced rather than the quantity' (Reuter, 2008). The many unintended consequences of drug prohibition have been counter-productive and, in most instances, instead of fixing the problem they have made it much worse. It is difficult to think of any positive consequences associated with drug prohibition unless we count the increased employment on personal, commercial and domestic security. There has been a trend everywhere for shops and offices nowadays to employ security guards in a bid to stop shoplifting and burglary, and many people now invest in domestic burglar alarms. Mexican spending on security has become a $1 billion a year boom industry. In 2009 there was a rise of 11 per cent in spending on alarm systems, bodyguards and risk consultants, and security spending increased by 33 per cent along the US–Mexican border (*Guardian*, 2010).

The war on drugs has cost a fortune to wage and has been won by drugs. Those who want to use drugs do so, risking their heath and freedom. Those who want to make money out them do so, more or less with impunity, by corrupting states, engaging in violent turf wars and, in some cases, funding terror and insurgency along the way. Why then, despite abject failure, does drug prohibition persist? This will be the subject of the next chapter.

6
Why Persist With a Failed Policy?

What have we learned from a hundred years of drug prohibition? We have learned that you can't buck the market: the drug markets work, prohibition does not. A fortune has been spent around the world on anti-drugs education and propaganda, on the treatment of addicts, and on eradication programmes, alternative development schemes and law enforcement, but the drugs tide continues to rise. Jails across the world are full of drug offenders, signalling that the promised deterrent effects of severe penalties facing users, dealers and traffickers are insufficient. The world is awash with recreational drugs, and the variety of drugs available continues to increase. Each time a new designer drug finds its way to the consumer, as in the recent case of methedrone, it is banned and a new one takes its place. Each time a trafficker or dealer is arrested, another appears. Drugs control has been securitized and militarized into an international war on drugs, but the enemy, like the devil, still has the best tunes. Melanie Reid sums up the situation: 'we can . . . ban methedrone, and with it the whole family of cathinones, we can ban the entire generation of derivatives that will surely follow from China, or indeed the generation after that. But nothing we do will alter the central, inescapable fact that people take drugs because they enjoy them' (Reid, 2010).

We have also learned that the 'drug problem' is at best shorthand for a long list of interconnected problems. The nature of the problem varies according to the drug in question, the way in which it is used and its affordability to the user. But these problems are hugely complicated and increased by the policy of prohibition which was supposed to fix the drug problem in the first place.

The prospect of a drug-free world is attractive to many, but it makes assumptions about human nature that do not seem to fit well with their actual behaviour. The idea of a drug-free world assumes that the law can prevent people from doing something they really want to do. The fact is that people's desire to use drugs can be frustrated, but not greatly deterred, by prohibition. Banning drugs assumes that most people are anti-drugs, and it does not take account of a whole range of unintended and unwelcome consequences that prohibition itself brings.

On the fiftieth anniversary of the UN 1961 Single Convention on Narcotic Drugs and the fortieth anniversary of Richard Nixon's declaration of the drug war (11 June 1971), the recently formed Global Commission on Drug Policy published 'On Drugs' (preceded by the word 'war' crossed out), calling for a 'paradigm shift' in drugs policy. The Commission, which is composed of some past political heavyweights including Former UN Secretary General Kofi Annan, former presidents of Mexico (Ernesto Zedillo), Brazil (Fernando Henrique) and Colombia (César Gaviria), as well as the business-man Richard Branson, the former US Federal Reserve chairman Paul Volcker, and the former US Secretary of State, George Schultz, and one currently serving prime minister, George Papandreou of Greece, claims that the war on drugs has failed and 'fundamental reforms in National and global drug control policies are urgently needed' (Global Commission on Drug Policy, 2011). The publication of the report has contributed to what is now becoming a clamour for change in international drug policy. It has provided greater awareness of and leadership to what, over the last decade or so, have been a few isolated voices crying in the wilderness. Tom Lloyd, the former chief constable of Cambridgeshire, has described the drug war as a waste of time: 'despite all the money and effort poured into the so-called "war on drugs", the inexorable spread of drugs and the accompany-ing damage is a powerful testament to failure. What we are doing is not only very expensive and misdirected activity, but actively counter-productive and harmful' (Lloyd, 2009). Antonia Senior argues along similar lines. She says it is obvious 'that the war on drugs has been lost . . . There has been no definitive battle, but there have been millions of small defeats and the victims of the war are everywhere: the users, the collateral victims, those that addicts rob to pay for a fix, children trafficked to work on cannabis farms, thousands dead in Mexico, British and US soldiers killed in Afghanistan by weapons paid for from drug profits' (Senior, 2009). Norm Stamper, a former Seattle police chief, says we spent a trillion dollars prosecuting the war on drugs and asks 'what do we have to show for it? Drugs are more readily available, at lower prices and higher levels of potency. It's a dismal failure' (Stamper, cit. Engel, 2009). Tim Hollis, the chief constable of Humberside police and the current chair of Britain's Association of Chief Police Officers' drugs committee, has endorsed calls for the decriminalization of cannabis for personal use. He does not want to criminalize young people with small quantities of cannabis. He also argues that financial constraints on the police make it impossible to arrest everyone caught with designer drugs bought on line (Townsend, 2010a). It is noteworthy that it is those tasked with enforcing prohibition whose voices are most prominent in the clamour calling for change. The police face the failure of the policy on a daily basis and see its negative impact on young people in particular. In addition to the growing number of individual voices calling for change, there are also a growing number of pressure groups, such as the Transform Drug Policy Foundation, which advocate legalization and regulation of all drugs here in Britain, and there are numerous groups in America pressing for the legalization of marijuana, or, in the case of the Drug Policy Alliance, the legalization of all drugs.

Why, despite the swelling criticisms of prohibition and the drug war, do we continue to wage a war which is neither winnable nor affordable? Why is it that politicians, who extol the virtues of evidence-based policy, seem happy to leave drug policy as an almost evidence-free zone? Around the world governments continue to defend a policy that has failed on all measures: drug use is not contained let alone stopped, levels of crime have risen, the health of addicts has worsened and the safety of society has diminished. This chapter considers the answers to this question. It does so by examining ideology, fear, expediency, bureaucratic inertia and the vested interests that stand in the way of policy change. It should be noted at the beginning that these categories overlap and interact and that political actors may be motivated by several of them or all of them at once.

Ideological explanations

Despite popular belief, drug policies have little to do with science, health risk or harm (McQueen, 2010). To diehard prohibitionists drug prohibition is more akin religion than to science. It is based on the belief that drugs are sinful, and this leaves no room for compromise. Drug prohibition is a moral imperative. The war against drugs is evidence based, but the evidence means different things to different people. To the anti-prohibitionists, and to some of those who advocate harm reduction, evidence of failure is a signal to stop and reappraise the policy. To the staunch prohibitionists who view drug use not only as a source of problems but as an evil in itself, the failure of prohibition is evidence of the need for even greater effort and more resources to be poured into making prohibition work. It is this kind of belief that informs the American approach, and America has successfully internationalized it in practice, if not in principle. Drugs corrupt the individual and undermine society, especially those societies with a Protestant work ethic and a belief that a traditional family is essential to social cohesion and a thriving capitalist economy. Ronald Reagan summed up the American view when he said: 'drug abuse is a repudiation of everything that America is' (Reagan, 1986). Drugs are evil. The only possible response to evil is prohibition. This straightforward moral view of prohibition sees the war on drugs as a war of good against evil, and it has the advantage that it can easily accommodate the failure of prohibition. The war against evil is good in itself, regardless of its success or failure. If the devil keeps winning battles, that is no reason for giving up. If there are more, not less drugs on the street, then you re-double your efforts. All wars cause collateral damage. ,Winning the drug war may not be in sight but it is still worth fighting. Any retreat in the drugs war would be to admit defeat. Drugs are subversive and to make matters worse, most of them are foreign. They are the enemy that has crossed our borders like an invading army that must be defeated. Elliot Abrams, when he was Assistant Secretary of State for Inter-American Affairs, articulated this view when he said that the drug problem 'is not a health problem, not just a foreign aid problem, not just a police problem. It is a moral challenge and a national security matter. It threatens democracy in our hemisphere and children in our homes' (Abrams, 1986).

For those firmly in the ideological camp, the prohibition of drugs is concerned with beliefs and values. Evidence of the failure of prohibition is evidence of the need to redouble the effort. Kathy Gyngell, for example, talks about 'the phoney war on drugs'. She accepts that all sorts of policies are in place to tackle drugs but argues that here in Britain punishment is not a deterrent against the use and trade in drugs because, while it is severe in principle, in practice severe sentences are rarely handed out (Gyngell, 2009). Simon Heffer agrees. He argues that we should get tough on drugs rather than legalize them. He says that drug dealers, and indeed drug users, are criminals. People continue to commit drug crimes 'not because we have unduly stringent policies against crime but because they are not stringent enough'. He continues, 'legalisation is not the answer, but getting nasty might be'. Heffer claims that 'old lags' confirm that drugs 'circulate freely in most prisons and that the authorities turn a blind eye to them in the interest of a quiet life' (Heffer, 2010). He concludes that this illustrates the moral failure of our drugs policy. In a similar vein Mev Brown's explanation for why the war on drugs is futile is that waging it is not really anybody's top priority. Drawing examples from the Lothian and Borders Police Authority, he points out that in June 2009 there were 64 Scottish Serious Crime and Drug Enforcement Agency officers in the force. He contrasts this with 45 traffic wardens and 139 parking attendants working in the same area at the same time. 'So we have 184 personnel tackling the social scourge of illegal parking compared to 64 officers dealing with illegal drugs, among their other duties including serious fraud, people trafficking, money laundering and electronic crimes' (Brown, 2010).

To the diehard prohibitionists, to concede that prohibition has not worked and never will demands a moral transformation and the denial of a cultural anxiety about drugs that can be traced back at least to Homer. The drug problem in essence is their very existence at all. The drug problem must be dealt with by a combination of abstinence and the eradication of supply. In this reading of the situation policy failure is interpreted as a problem of enforcement (Buxton, 2006, 111). Users are conceptualized as dope fiends, at best weak and in need of treatment, at worst morally depraved criminals who should be punished.

Fear

The fear that lies behind the drugs problem is that all users would become hopeless and dangerous addicts if drug use became legal. This fear helps to sustain the prohibition regime. While not all of the countries that have signed up to the UN Conventions accept the moral arguments for prohibition, even those that hold less die-hard views fear a 'free for all' legalization of drugs. 'Things could be worse' is the mantra of those who recognize that prohibition has not worked, but that it may have helped to contain some of the damage. Antonio Maria Costa, the former Executive Director of the UNODC, warns that if drugs were to be legalized then a world epidemic of addiction would follow. He argues that the effectiveness of the UN Conventions' restraint on both the supply of, and demand for, drugs is undeniable and he draws comparisons between tobacco and heroin to substantiate his argument. Less than one per cent of the world's population is addicted to heroin and 5 per cent of the world's population use drugs at least once a year. But 30 per cent use tobacco, implying, therefore, that if heroin was legal like tobacco, there would be a similar rise in use (Costa, 2010). Politicians seem to reflect the views of publics in general, that drug use is a pressing problem, although these views are likely to have been stoked up by media hysteria about drugs (see, for example, Sare, 2011). This could, of course, change, and perhaps it has already done so, as those young people for whom recreational drugs use have become 'normal' take up jobs in the media, influence politicians or become politicians themselves. Politicians worry about what the world would be like if all drugs were legal. They listen to what the media tells them and the media helps to shape the views of the electorate. Public discourse is driven by the media and by politicians anxious to justify the status quo. As noted earlier, George Papandreou, the prime minister of Greece, is the only politician in office to serve on, and endorse the call for a change in policy advocated the Global Commission on Drug Policy. Mike Levi, reflecting on the likelihood of changes in prohibition policy, argues that 'however good an ideal it might be in the abstract it would take a more mature political and media conversation about it before it is likely to happen. Always keep a-hold of nurse, for fear of finding something worse, that's where we are now' (Levi, cit Engel, 2009). Clearly if mass addiction was the outcome of legalization, it could not last forever. If, as now in welfare states, addicts lived off welfare benefits then who would produce the tax revenue? What would happen to families? What would happen to society, to Hobbes' 'commodious living'? It can, after all, be plausibly argued that prohibition, with its criminal penalties and its propaganda about the evils and dangers of drugs, does in fact deter some potential users. To those who fear the worst, prohibition may be the least worst option. My own students have assured me that many of their friends had switched from ecstasy and cocaine to methedrone, and others had tried methedrone, because it was legal and there was therefore no risk of getting a criminal record. Their views appear to be reinforced by research into drug use in the British Army. Drugs tests on soldiers showed that cocaine use fell by 50 per cent in 2008–9 when the methedrone craze what at its height, prior to it being banned (UKDPC, 2009). Peter Reuter reminds us of the difficulties of judging the success of prohibition, because its success is about outcomes that did not occur (Reuter, 2009a, 1). Prohibition may have succeeded in holding back the flood.

Expediency

Expediency contributes to the continuation of international drug prohibition. Those countries that are already recipients of American aid may mutter about breaking the ranks of drug prohibition but rarely do so, or if so, not for long. In Mexico, President Vincente Fox came to office promising to relax the drug laws. He immediately came under American pressure to change his mind. Few observers were surprised when, two years later, he retreated from this position when faced with ratifying a bill decriminalizing drug use and possession. He explained that his original intention was to direct drug offenders into treatment instead of prison, and he blamed the legislature for changing the spirit of his reforms (Dellios, 2006). The drug problem for Nigeria when it was decertified by America, – and therefore denied US aid – was not the problem of the drugs themselves but a problem of needing American aid and being coerced into taking action against the drug transit business that used Nigeria as a staging post in the trafficking of drugs to Europe. Nowadays some of the former producer countries are themselves experiencing problems associated with drug use at home, but until recently their drug problems were largely caused by the fact that their most valuable cash crop was prohibited. However, as poor countries in receipt of American aid, expediency dictated that they at least pretend to enforce prohibition.

Bureaucratic inertia

Bureaucratic inertia plays a part in sustaining policies long past their usefulness. International drug prohibition of one kind or another has now been with us for a hundred years. This has allowed plenty of time for a whole range of institutions devoted to prohibition to develop at local, national, regional and international levels, whose main *raison d'être* is overseeing, monitoring and reporting on drug prohibition. We have already noted that drug agencies liaise with a whole range of 'service providers' from local doctors, to substance misuse nurses, counsellors, child welfare teams, social workers, to enforcement agencies like the police, the courts, the probation service and others. Drug bureaucracies are multiplied many times over in advanced welfare states and also in less developed countries. In Britain, for example, the National Treatment Agency was created as part of the 1997 Labour government's ten-year drug strategy, 'Tackling Drugs Together'. Its job was to monitor the quality of treatment purchased locally, to disseminate good practice and to get 100 per cent more drug users into treatment by 2008. It did achieve this latter target, although the quality of treatment delivered has been subject to much criticism. In bureaucratic terms it was highly successful. It began with a staff of 30, and by the end of 2008 it had a staff of 150 and operating costs of £14.5 million a year (Gyngell, 2010). There are also burgeoning drug bureaucracies at regional level, including those of the European Union, the Caribbean countries, and the Andean countries, that co-ordinate prohibition in member states and feed data into a range of UN bodies set up to administer and monitor drug prohibition.

Like most bureaucracies, the drug bureaucracy is resistant to change. It is not, however, a monolith. Not all of these bodies sing the same prohibition tune. In some countries there are different attitudes at different levels of the drug bureaucracy. The drug policy of national governments may be at odds with the policy on the front line or at street level. British drug policy placed an emphasis on harm minimization (Home Office 2005). How was this to be implemented? In practice, this is far from clear. If a police officer apprehends someone in possession of a class A drug, should they charge them with the offence and confiscate the substance? This might minimize harm if the user thinks better of using and is willing to be directed into treatment, but in the short term the user may score to replace the confiscated drugs and cause the further harm of robbing someone else to fund it (Lister et al., 2008). There are also conflicts between the policies of different countries, even if they have signed up to the UN Conventions. Sweden, for example, is highly critical of the liberal drug policy adopted by the Dutch. Sweden has a more ideological, zero tolerance approach. It makes no distinction between hard and soft drugs, whereas in the Netherlands the situation is much more nuanced, with drug use being seen as part of ordinary life. Instead it seeks to minimize the damage drug use may inflict on individuals and society. To this end cannabis coffee houses are tolerated and there are clear distinctions between hard and soft drugs, and between using and dealing. There are also divisions within the UN itself. The World Health Organization presses for harm minimization in respect of drugs. It regards poverty and the spread of AIDS as a far more serious threat to mankind than drug use, and therefore prefers that needle exchanges and accurate information on good practice should be the key to drug policies. The UNODC however is financed predominantly by American money and steeped in American ideology, and has therefore so far emphasized zero tolerance and supply-side policies (see Hartnoll, 1998).

Bureaucracies excel at perpetuating and manipulating the system in which they function. Cindy Fazey, a former employee of the UNODC, describes the UN institutions as being populated by self-interested and risk-averse bureaucrats. They are often less concerned with the public good than with the well-being of themselves and their bureaucratic allies (Fazey, 2003). Bureaucrats are reluctant to step out of line in case they inhibit their promotion or in case they get posted to some distant UN delegation far away from the comforts of Vienna. Fazey argues that because of short term tenure, 'punishment postings' and the power of the paymaster (in particular the US) 'people are often more concerned with politicking to keep their jobs than actually doing them' (Fazey, 2003). So the UN drug bureaucracy, the very centre of the international prohibition regime, has little incentive to change anything.

At national, regional and international levels, prohibition creates acres of institutional turf to be hotly defended against internal enemies and against change. Except for the violence, it compares easily with the turf wars of the traffickers and dealers it confronts. David

Bewley-Taylor describes how in 1932 the incoming Democratic administration in America considered dismantling the Federal Bureau of Narcotics. Harry Anslinger, the Bureau Head in 1930, defended his empire by exaggerating the drug threat and linking it directly to US national security interests (Bewley-Taylor, 1999). This was at a time when drug prohibition was in its infancy. The prohibition bureaucracy had not yet grown into the giant whose inertia now stifles anyone trying to introduce changes of any sort, let alone the legalization of drugs. When Barack Obama was elected in 2008, he spoke in favour of toning down the 'drug war' rhetoric. However, this has not been translated into much policy change at the front. Coletta Youngers argues that there have been some modest initiatives in drug policy that mark a departure from past approaches: 'their effective implementation hinges on the administrations willingness to fund them adequately. So far, the Obama administration has not shown the political will to take on the bureaucratic battles such a shift of funding priorities would entail' (Youngers, 2011, 9).

Vested interests

Vested interests are everywhere in the politics of prohibition and they seek ways of sustaining the policy regime from which they benefit. The prohibition bureaucracy is only the largest of a whole host of bureaucratized 'charitable' and private institutions locked into providing treatment for drugs and the enforcement of prohibition. These have become an industrial–treatment–enforcement-complex on a world scale. They treat addicts at private and public expense. They develop drug testing kits, substitute drugs, equipment for safe injecting, drugs education packages and so on. These providers are well intentioned and have the interests of the addict at heart, but their jobs and profits come from the drug control industry. In Britain, for example, the emphasis on harm reduction drug policies had, until the change of government in 2010, prompted widespread reliance on prescribing the heroin substitute, methadone, itself an addictive drug, to approximately half of the country's 330,000 heroin addicts. There is a strong financial incentive for the drug companies, doctors and pharmacies to support the continued use of this treatment. According to Neil McKeganey, a leading critic of the mass prescription of methadone, drug companies make millions from producing methadone. General practitioners in many parts of the country get paid approximately £220 per methadone patient per year, pharmacists get £200 administration fees plus about £1.50 per administered dose (McKeganey, cit Sanderson and Fishburn, 2010). Reckitts, the pharmaceutical firm which produces Suboxone, has seen its profits rise from £118 million in 2007 to £531 million in 2010, largely as a result of suboxone becoming the preferred treatment for heroin addiction in America. These profits are likely to continue to rise now that the British government has also changed its preferred treatment policy from methadone and switched to prescribing subutex, which is also produced by Reckitts (Bowers, 2011).

There are also a range of vested interests on the enforcement side who supply chemicals, hardware and teams for eradication programmes, the police and the security agencies. An end to prohibition is unlikely to be welcomed by what Mary O'Grady describes as the 'drug-warrior industry' those 'private sector and government bureaucracies devoted to "enforcement" have an enormous economic incentive to keep the war going' (O'Grady, 2010). There are alternative development advisers and planners, conference organizers, academics and medical practitioners who research and write about drugs. There are even lobby groups which receive public funding for lobbying the government on drug policy on behalf of service providers who also benefit from public funds. DrugScope, for example, the leading drugs information charity in the UK, receives part of its funding from the British government in exchange for representing the different views of service providers, and to a lesser extent drug users, to the government, and helping to interpret changes in government policy to the wider community. These are all part of the wider prohibition industry, the beneficiaries of the policy and ultimately of the taxpayer. These bodies may be sources of initiatives, but these mainly involve minor changes, such as the emphasis on substitute prescribing rather than abstinence or community sentences rather than prison.

In Britain, the outspoken Labour MP Paul Flynn says: 'we're building up a huge drug prohibition establishment of people with a vested interest in continuing the present policies of prohibition, which keep them in employment … It's a self-feeding empire that continually swells and becomes more bloated' (Flynn, 2009). This self-feeding and bloated establishment already exists.

It is clear that a lot of self-interested groups beside the traffickers and dealers have a direct interest in drugs remaining illegal and have a lot to lose if the policy were to be abandoned. Those in the massive drug prohibition industry receive millions from the prohibition dividend.

The attempt to prohibit drugs on a global basis is not based on any evidence that it can actually be achieved. In fact, most of the available evidence points to the failure of prohibition, but as stated earlier the policy of prohibition is driven by moral assertion. Prohibition is based on deeply held beliefs about the good life. The good life is about liberty, not licence. It is about liberty to choose good over evil. Liberty is not conceived as the liberty to enslave oneself to a drug. Ideas such as these are deeply embedded in American politics and it is America that has tried to shape a drug world in its own image. From this perspective there is little point in even considering evidence that prohibition cannot deliver a drug-free world. The important thing is to try to make it more likely that those who are weak enough to fall into temptation will be deterred and have their resolve strengthened by making it hard to get the stuff in the first place.

This philosophy then becomes reinforced by political, bureaucratic and business interests that benefit from the status quo of prohibition. Now, at the start of a new century, there are forces for change. The expression 'international community' conveys an impression of unity. However, for the less ideological drug warriors, this international prohibition regime has become an obstacle to more local solutions to particular rather than global aspects of the drug problem. Prohibition has become a straitjacket that deters experiment to find these local solutions (Hartnoll, 1998).

Are we then witnessing the beginning of the end of drug prohibition? This is a question for the next chapter which will identify the national and international pressures for change that may eventually lead to the fall of the ancient prohibition regime.

7
Is the Attempt to Prohibit Drugs Coming to An End?

The international drug prohibition regime may not be about to disintegrate but there are an increasing number of cracks appearing. This trend of a growing restlessness and discomfort about the failure and costs of international prohibition is being egged on and publicized by a growing rank of the great and the good (see, for example, the Report of the Global Commission on Drug Policy 2011 and Birdwill et al., 2011). The belief that prohibition would fix the drug problem has been undermined by the facts. The growing sense of disquiet is predicated on the fact that no research shows that tougher enforcement, more prevention or more treatments have resulted in a substantial reduction in the number of users or addicts (Reuter, 2009b). In 2008 a World Health Organization (WHO) study covering 17 countries found no link between the strictness of prohibition and the level of drug consumption (WHO/UNICRI, 2008).

Rather than reducing drug harm, prohibition has actually increased it dramatically. John Gray sums up the situation thus: 'from Liverpool to Moscow, Tokyo to Detroit, a punitive regime of prohibition has turned streets into battlefields, while drug use has remained embedded in the way we live. The anti-drug crusade will go down as among the greatest follies of modern times' (Gray, 2009).

In 1998 a United Nations General Assembly Special Session (UNGASS) proclaimed a decade against drugs, but any hopes that a drug-free world could be created in ten years have been dashed. The 1990s and 2000s turned out to be a decade *of* drugs, a decade in which the number of drug users and the variety of recreational drugs available increased dramatically all over the world. The 1998–2008 period saw global potential opium production increase by 78 per cent, from 4,346 to 7,754 metric tons and global potential cocaine production by 5 per cent from 825 to 865 metric tons. The figures for cannabis and for ATSs are difficult to come by because of the decentralization of production (World Drug Report, 2010, 12). We do know that cannabis, both herbal and resin, continues to be the world's most popular illegal drug (ibid.). We also know that the tide of ATSs continues to rise. The past decade has witnessed an expansion of organized crime linked to the drug trade, an increase in the number of insurgent groups cashing in on the easy money obtainable from the drug trade, widespread drug-related violence, corruption of politicians, bureaucracies, judicial systems, police and even armies, and the subversion of economic institutions which turn a blind eye to money laundering. Many would agree with Milton Friedman when he asserted 'drugs are a tragedy for addicts. But criminalizing their use converts that tragedy into a disaster for society' (Friedman, 1990).

The overwhelming evidence that drug prohibition has failed is hard to ignore, except by the drug prohibition diehards, who will see in it a further motive for a further re-doubling of the prohibition efforts, as if there is no such thing as throwing good money after bad. Drug prohibition has become more difficult to defend since those who took drugs and lived to tell the tale with little or no harm, have become the political leaders of today: Bill Clinton, George W. Bush and Barack Obama are just the most prominent. The days of the prohibition, or at least of the criminalization, of drugs have probably been numbered since the children of the middle classes began to be imprisoned for drug offences. It has also become much harder to sustain prohibition as the developing countries mature economically and politically and question the cultural and economic dominance of the West. The rich West demands that they eradicate their best cash crop, accept the invasion of anti-drug teams spraying their land and their peasant farmers with noxious chemicals in the name of saving the rich, indulged, bored youth of the western consumer countries (net drug importers) who do not in any case wish to be saved from the pleasures of recreational drugs. Why should the coca chewers of the Andes be forced to give up drug use that has formed part of their culture for hundreds of years and that has both spiritual and medicinal functions? There is also the inconsistency and hypocrisy of condemning the use of cannabis, which predominantly has a soporific, calming effect, or ecstasy, which makes users love all those around them and dance all night, while condoning the use of alcohol which is all too often accompanied by mayhem in towns and cities as well as hidden violence within the home. The drug war, with its growing number of casualties, has become increasingly difficult to defend. In Mexico, 28,000 have died in Mexico's drug war in the last four years compared with 1,565 coalition troops in the same period in Afghanistan (icasualties.org/oes). The drugs war has become even more difficult to defend now that those casualties are spreading across the Mexican border to America, the home of prohibition and the drug war (O'Neill 2010; Maddox, 2010). But the drugs war's casualties are not only measured in terms of those who have been killed; its casualties are also measured in the thousands of (mostly) young people who have had their lives marred by criminal records, time spent in prison and being treated as social outcasts. Lastly, in the middle of a world credit crunch it is difficult to justify the trillions of dollars spent globally on a policy that has not only failed to deliver but has also produced so much collateral damage.

It is little wonder that, nationally and internationally, the policy of drug prohibition is being challenged and, in some places, changed. Martin Jelsma, reflecting on the current state of international prohibition, notes that 'over the last decade rapidly widening cracks have begun to split the global drug control consensus' and he thinks that this will lead to the emergence of 'more pragmatic and less punitive approaches to the drugs issue in the future' (Jelsma, 2011). This chapter will examine the cracks that are appearing in the international prohibition regime. It will identify the sources of the challenges and the nature of the changes that have already been made and question whether they can be accommodated within the UN anti-drug Conventions. It will end by reflecting on the kinds of changes which are being introduced and discussed, and ask if some half-measure such as the decriminalization of cannabis is feasible on its own or whether it is, as critics claim, a Trojan horse for drug legalization. Before this it will first be useful to clarify what is understood by some of the key terms: harm reduction; decriminalization; depenalization; legalization; regulation.

- *Harm reduction* refers to a number of policies and practices which are intended to reduce the adverse health, social and economic consequences of the use of prohibited psychoactive drugs to users, their families and the community, without necessarily ending drug consumption (Blickman and Jelsma, 2009). It includes such practices as prescribing substitute drugs to heroin users, dispensing clean needles, the police disrupting street dealing, and blue lighting in public toilets to prevent drug users injecting in such premises. In Britain the Rolleston Report of 1926 introduced the idea of harm reduction policies. It advocated medicalizing the drug problem by prescribing to addicts the particular drug to which they were addicted.

- *Decriminalization* is a kind of half-way house in which an activity remains unlawful but is no longer treated as a criminal offence. Those breaking this kind of law do not receive a criminal record. In some countries they may receive a fine under the heading of administrative law.
- *Depenalization* is much the same as the above. In this case the activity remains a criminal offence but it is no longer punishable with a custodial sentence.
- *Legalization* removes an activity from the sphere of criminal law. In the case of drugs, the use, possession, cultivation, production and trade would no longer be against the law.
- *Regulation* means something is subject to controls such as those specified under the terms of a licence, something along the lines of the current restrictions on the sale and use of tobacco and alcohol.

There is a considerable confusion between decriminalization and depenalization (Blickman and Jelsma, 2009). Certainly, as will be seen below, the idea of decriminalization seems less clear on closer inspection than it appears at first glance.

The sources of challenge and change

In Britain, this year (2011), to mark the fortieth anniversary of the key anti-drug legislation, the 1971 Misuse of Drugs Act, a group composed of the great, the good, the rich and the famous, signed a letter to the Prime Minister. This letter called on the coalition government to undertake 'a swift and transparent review of effectiveness of the current drug policies' and 'should such a review of the evidence demonstrate the failure of the current position' they would call for 'the decriminalization of drug possession' (Release, 2011). The signatories included the former Home Office minister with responsibility for drugs, Bob Ainsworth, MP, journalist Polly Toynbee, actors Dame Judi Dench, Julie Christie and Kathy Burke, the musician Sting, the businessman Sir Richard Branson, four former chief constables, three members of Parliament, the film director Mike Leigh and several academics, lawyers and journalists. Their letter pointed out that in the previous year (2010) nearly 80,000 people in the UK, most of whom were young, black or poor, were found guilty or cautioned for the possession of an illegal drug. They argue that drug policy is 'costly for taxpayers and damaging for communities' (ibid.). The *Daily Mail* responded predictably with the headline 'Luvvies for Legalisation: You're Being Naive in the Extreme, Celebrities Told after Drugs Plea to PM' (Doyle, 2011). The response from the Home Office was also predictable; it ruled out any change. The spokesman for the Home Office said 'we have no intention of liberalizing our drug laws. Drugs are illegal because they are harmful – they destroy lives and cause untold misery to families and communities . . . giving people the green light to possess drugs through decriminalization is clearly not the answer' (cit. Travis, 2011). David Cameron, who, like Barack Obama, had flirted with radical drug law reform before taking office (see Select Committee on Home Affairs Report, 2002), seems to have retreated to the default position of prohibition, 'no ifs, no buts'. The Home Office spokesman reiterated the British government's position: 'we are taking action through tough enforcement, both inland and abroad, alongside temporary banning powers and robust treatment programmes that lead people into drug free recovery' (cit. Travis, 2011).

This public and critical outburst against current drug policy in Britain coincided with the Global Commission on Drug Policy's call for a policy rethink on the fortieth anniversary of the Drug War and the fiftieth anniversary of the 1961 UN Convention on Narcotic Drugs. These protests marked the latest stage of what has become an increasingly public and international critique of drug prohibition.

In the name of 'harm reduction', a growing number of countries have begun to break ranks with the policy of strict prohibition. The Netherlands was probably the first to do so, and it is certainly well known for its liberal attitude towards drug use. Contrary to popular belief, drugs are neither legal nor decriminalized in the Netherlands. In the 1976 Dutch policy makers, on the recommendation of the

Baan Commission, adopted a drug policy based on harm reduction. They decided to adopt separate strategies for the markets for hard drugs such as heroin, and those for softer drugs like cannabis. Cannabis users were allowed to buy small amounts of the drug for personal use in specially licensed Cannabis coffee shops, the so-called 'cannabis cafés', most of which are in Amsterdam. The strict international repressive norm still applied to the supply side of the drug market. The possession of cannabis technically remains an offence, but the guidelines mean that possession is rarely prosecuted. The Netherlands has devised a compromise between the drug-war hawks and the legalizing doves (Parliamentary Research Branch, 2009). The rationale for this policy is that users of soft drugs will not be exposed to the hard drugs scene and the dealers of hard drugs. The policy has had mixed results. Cannabis use in the Netherlands has declined and the more liberal attitude towards drugs, including facilities to allow clubs to test the composition of ecstasy tablets, has resulted in a lower rate of drug deaths (see European Monitoring Centre for Comparative Drug and Drug Addiction, 2010). The division of the drug market has been a limited success. Those who visit such cafés report that other drugs are easily obtained in and around the cafés. There has also been growing discontent about the growth of drug tourism. While some Dutch dislike the country's reputation as the place to go if you want to use drugs with impunity, others criticize neighbouring countries which continue to hold a hard line on drugs, fully aware that their young people cross the border to get a better, safer deal in the Netherlands (Wakerfield, 2010). There are currently moves to make the cannabis coffee shops more restrictive. One proposal has been to require the shops to become clubs open only to members. It is argued that this would curtail drug tourism. The mayor of Eindhoven, Ron van Gyzel, argues that if the coffee shops were turned into clubs it would solve the problem not only of drug tourists but also of the problem of illegal supply. The clubs could take advantage of the fact that individuals are allowed to grow up to five cannabis plants for their own use. He suggests the clubs could grow up to five plants for each of their members (Dutch News.nl, 2010).

The Netherlands may have led the way in the 1970s, but the 1980s saw a more general shift in the drug policy towards harm reduction. America continued to pursue a hard enforcement line, but many other countries began to regard containing the spread of HIV/AIDS as a priority over curbing drug use (Berridge, 1991). The link between the spread of HIV/AIDS and injecting drugs use became incontrovertible, and in contrast to the link between AIDS and the gay community, drug users seemed much more likely to infect heterosexuals. So AIDS helped the addicts, when countries like Britain rushed to provide clean syringes, clear instructions on safe injecting techniques and exhortations not to share equipment. The Home Office stopped keeping a register of heroin users, partly in the hope that more people would come forward for either treatment for addiction or to participate in the needle exchange scheme.

Switzerland was the next country to challenge the UN prohibition regime. In the 1990s it reviewed its drug policies and decided to try what was in the past referred to as the 'British system' and in its modern reincarnation is called Heroin Assisted Treatment (HAT). Under this programme heroin addicts are provided with pharmaceutical heroin in the hope that it will reduce the medical harms arising from overdoses and impure drugs, and the social harms of drug-related crime. The experiment has been judged a success, and not only by policy makers. In a referendum in 2008, 68 per cent of voters were in favour of continuing this policy. Other countries, including Australia, Canada, Germany, the Netherlands, and Spain, have also experimented with prescribing heroin as part of the repertoire of drug treatments. Britain is again tentatively making pharmaceutical heroin available for a small number of the more recalcitrant long-term users and Norway is also now proposing to try this kind of treatment (for a detailed study of HAT see Hallam, 2010b).

In the Andes there is also a growing willingness to challenge the US/UN prohibition hegemony. Colombia, Peru and Bolivia have spent decades on the drug war's front line. They have endured constant American interventions in their internal affairs, under the guise of helping to fight a drug trade that they regard as much less of a problem than does America. Bolivia has cooperated with the Americans in its fight against coca cultivation for the cocaine market, but it remains resistant to UN pressure to prohibit coca and the practice of coca chewing. The 25-year period of grace it was granted in the UN Single Convention (1961) has now passed and Bolivia has been under pressure to outlaw coca. In 2005 Evo Morales, a former coca farmer, was elected Bolivian president in part on a promise that he would legalize and modernize the coca leaf industry. At the time of writing Morales' 'Coca Yes Cocaine No' campaign has not succeeded in persuading the UNODC, but coca chewing continues in both Bolivia and Peru and the cultivation of coca for a variety of non-cocaine coca products remains legal. In June this year (2011) Morales announced to the UNODC his intention to withdraw from the 1961 Single Convention on Narcotic Drugs, to enable Bolivia to negotiate an exemption protocol to allow coca to remain legal in Bolivia, and thereafter to rejoin the Convention.

The cracks in the international consensus about drugs are widening and they are no longer confined to a liberal attitude in the Netherlands and the growing acceptance of needle exchanges and limited heroin prescribing elsewhere. In 2001 Portugal became the first country to decriminalize all drug use, not only for softer drugs like cannabis. Drugs are still illegal in Portugal. The penalties for people caught dealing or trafficking drugs are unchanged, dealers are still pros-ecuted, imprisoned and fined, but those caught in possession of small quantities of drugs for their own use, up to ten days' supply, are not prosecuted. Instead they are directed, by citations issued by the police, to special panels composed of medical professionals, lawyers and social workers whose purpose is to persuade the user to give up drugs. Evidence about how effective this policy has so far been mixed (see Greenwald, 2009 for a full appraisal). Supporters point out that, contrary to dire predications, mayhem has not resulted and there has been no significant increase in drug use and no rush of drug tourists. In the first five years of the policy the number of deaths from street overdoses dropped from around 400 to 290 annually and there has also been a drop in HIV cases linked to illegal drug use from 1,400 in 2000 to 400 in 2006 (Greenwald, 2009). Not everyone accepts this view. As might be expected, Dr Manuel Pinto Coelho, chairman of the Association for a Drug Free Portugal, argues that the Portuguese experience is being 'over-egged' and that, contrary to claims, 'decriminalization of drugs in Portugal did not decrease consumption'; instead, use increased by over 4 per cent (Coelho, 2010). Another cautionary note is sounded by Nigel Keegan, who points out that, according to the Special Registry of the National Institute for Forensic Medicine in Portugal, there has actually been an increase in drug-related deaths in Portugal since this policy was introduced, from 280 in 2001 to 314 in 2007 (Keegan, 2010).

Despite the mixed messages coming from Portugal, Spain and Italy have now introduced similar policies, and Spain actually encourages marijuana smokers to grow their own plants with a view to removing supply from the control of criminal gangs. Drug possession for personal use is no longer a criminal offence in Italy, the Czech Republic or the Baltic states and Argentina, Brazil, Venezuela and Ecuador seem likely to follow suit. Three former heads of state, César Gaviria of Colombia, Fernando Cardos of Brazil and Ernesto Zedillo of Mexico, have called for the legalization of cannabis and this kind of liberalization may eventually lead to decriminalization of drugs in those countries too. Even President Felipe Calderón of Mexico, currently America's closest drug war ally, is becoming wobbly about prohibition. A Mexican death toll to date of 28,000 in the last four years has persuaded even President Calderón to wonder if it is worth it. After the decriminalization of small quantities of cannabis for personal use, he has now launched a national debate on the question of decriminalizing drugs, and has called on his critics to help him to realign the government's approach to the drug war.

For the moment Britain is holding the line against drugs, although probably more in rhetoric than reality. Kathy Gyngell argues that Britain has had de facto decriminalization for the last ten years. She cites 'declining levels of custodial sentencing, directing of addicts into methadone maintenance, the sanguine response of the judge to Pete Doherty's attending court with Class A drugs in his pocket, the warnings instead of penalties for cannabis possession and the general blind eye on the tripling of cocaine use' (Gyngell, 2010). Kathy Gyngell and Neil McKeganey argue that 'drug decriminalization has become the new orthodoxy' and that it is 'an idea that has captured the broadsheets and has won the support of the great and the good' (Gyngell and McKeganey, 2011). Britain has certainly embraced the harm minimization agenda. In policy terms, this accounts for the introduction of the methadone maintenance programme, needle exchanges and the provision of more honest and accurate drug information. But the view expressed by Kathy Gyngell, and probably endorsed by some of the public and media, shows that the debate about drug prohibition, which ten years ago took place behind closed doors, if indeed it took place at all, has now been joined by a much wider public. When the Transform Drug Policy Foundation, a pressure group dedicated to the legalization and regulation of all drugs, was formed in 1997, it seemed to be far too radical and out of step with both elite and public opinion, but it is now rapidly becoming mainstream. In the autumn of 2009 the government's chief drugs adviser, Professor David Nutt, was sacked from his job as chairman of the Advisory Council on the Misuse of Drugs for publicly expressing his opinions on the comparative safety of legal and illegal drugs and for arguing that using ecstasy was less dangerous than horse riding (Slack, 2009). Now, in July 2010, Nicholas Green QC, chairman of the prestigious Bar Council, has argued that decriminalizing drugs would not lead to greater use and would actually cut crime. He pointed out that 'a growing body of comparative evidence suggests that decriminalizing personal use can have positive consequences, it can free up huge amounts of police resources, reduce crime and recidivism and improve public health' (cit. Dunt, 2010). In August Professor Ian Gilmore, the outgoing president of the Royal College of Physicians, accepting that it would end his presidency on a controversial note, gave his backing to the arguments of Nicholas Green. Colin Blakemore, a member of the UK Drug Policy Commission, says 'when pillars of the Establishment as solid as Sir Ian Gilmore, retiring president of the Royal College of Physicians and Nicholas Green QC the chairman of the UK Bar Council, talk of decriminalization, you know that the anti-war campaign is suddenly moving into the mainstream' (Blakemore, 2010). If we add to these voices those of a generation of parents and even grandparents who have themselves used drugs without harm, unless they were unlucky enough to get caught in possession of drugs and prosecuted, and the voices of a number of influential commentators in the quality press who endorse legalizing or decriminalizing drugs, the letter to the prime minister this year being the latest and most formal example, there are the makings of the kind of changing climate of opinion that may eventually lead to a more liberal approach in Britain. YouGov poll results published on 17 June 2011 suggest that opinion is moving towards support for changing the drug laws. It reported that more than 50 per cent of British people believe the government's approach to illegal drugs is ineffective. Only 8 per cent think that a drug-free society could ever be achieved. In the same survey 23 per cent of those polled believed marijuana should be legal, but a majority, 52 per cent, rejected drug legalization (YouGov, 2011).

Die-hard prohibitionists, however, are now confronting a much more worrying pressure for change, and it comes from the epicentre of the drug war itself, America. In the States the prohibition consensus is beginning to break down. Since Barack Obama became president, the emphasis of federal domestic drug policy has begun to shift away from strict enforcement towards harm reduction. His newly appointed drug czar, former Seattle police chief Gil Kerlikowske, has already dropped the term 'war on drugs' from his lexicon (Berger, 2009). In an editorial the *Observer* comments that in America 'the unthinkable is creeping into the realm of the plausible' (*Observer* editorial, 2010). It cites as supporting evidence the fact that several states have relaxed cannabis laws. This trend is being driven by a loose coalition of hard right libertarians who believe that free market liberty extends to drugs, and soft left baby-boomers who have probably used drugs themselves. America is beginning to accept that drug use is part of everyday life (*Observer* editorial, 2010). Sixteen states now permit the medical use of marijuana. Medical marijuana is already big business in California. Use of the drug is approved for a range of medical conditions including multiple sclerosis and 'any other illness for which marijuana provides relief', something of a carte blanche. It is even obtainable in the form of marijuana ice cream. Mike Harvey notes that there are already an estimated 21,000 marijuana dispensaries in California, outnumbering the Starbucks, McDonald's and 7-Eleven outlets and generating around $2.5 billion in cannabis sales and $220 million in sales tax (Harvey, 2009). The National Organization for Reform of Marijuana Laws (NORML) is hoping to capitalize on the recession which has made the prospect of legalizing and taxing marijuana a tempting prospect. Legalization was put to California's voters as proposition 19 in the mid-term elections this autumn (2010). George Soros, billionaire and long-term supporter of legalizing cannabis, donated $1million to the legalization campaign. He noted that: 'the mere fact of its being on the ballot has elevated and legitimized public discourse about marijuana' (Soros, cit. Goldberg, 2010). The proposition which would have allowed the cultivation, use and taxation of marijuana was defeated but the vote was 56:44. Richard Lee, founder of the Oakstadam University, a cannabis business school in the Bay Area of the city of Oakland, remains optimistic and argues that 45 per cent of people voting for it [legalization] makes it hard to lock people up for it' (cit. Harris, 2010). Where California leads other states will follow, even if more slowly. Medical use of marijuana is now permitted in 13 states and 9 more are in the processes of considering legislation to permit it. In Phoenix, Arizona, which recently decriminalized medical use of marijuana, a 'WeGrow' marijuana superstore is about to open. The 21,000 sq. ft store will sell a range of products especially designed for those wishing to cultivate marijuana, including, UV lights, root stimulators, fertilizer and pruning scissors (Gabbat, 2011). The federal government may also be starting to change. At the end of 2009 the US House of Representatives unanimously approved a bill which created an independent commission to review domestic and international drug policy. However, little has been heard from them so far. In 2009 the Justice Department announced that it would end the aggressive enforcement of federal drug laws in states that have adopted laws legalizing marijuana for medical purposes. Coletta Youngers points out, however, that it is the DEA which has the job of raiding medical marijuana facilities in states where they operate legally but contravene federal law. The DEA has 'publicly expressed disagreement with this policy shift . . . [and] has continued to carry out raids on such facilities' (Youngers, 2011).

Is this the beginning of the end of drug prohibition?

Do the challenges and changes mentioned above add up to the de facto end of the international prohibition regime? The UNODC and its monitory arm, the International Narcotics Control Board (INCB), have expressed disapproval of the less rigorous approach to enforcement that seems to have crept in under the banner of harm reduction. In 2009 the UNODC was forced to concede, on the insistence of 26 separate states, that the Conventions could be interpreted in such a way as to include endorsement of harm reduction practices such as needle exchanges. However, in 2009 the INCB annual report reprimanded Bolivia for continuing to permit coca chewing. In 2010 it criticized Argentina, Brazil and Mexico for moving in the direction of decriminalizing possession of drugs for personal consumption. Antonio Maria Costa, the retiring Executive Director of the UNODC, answered some of the growing chorus of critics of drug prohibition by pointing out that what has not been measured is the number of people who may have died or been harmed had drugs not been prohibited (Costa, 2009). He admits that there have been some policy failures, in particular the massive criminal black market, a failure to address questions of poverty and governance in key producer countries, and accepts that there is a need to emphasize the harm reduction aspect rather than enforcement when it comes to drug users (Costa, 2009). But, unsurprisingly, he continues to endorse prohibition although by emphasizing that 'drugs are controlled [*he does not say prohibited* – author's note] because they are dangerous'. He thereby conflates calls for legalization with calls for a drugs 'free-for-all', which few if any critics of prohibition have endorsed. Most of those who call for legalization also call for regulation; they expect that drugs will be regulated by a system of licensing. Antonio Maria Costa clearly recognizes that the climate of opinion is beginning to change. In 2010 he warned that legalizing drugs will result in a worldwide epidemic of addiction and argued that: 'in a world of free [legalized] drugs, the privileged rich can afford expensive treatment while the poor are condemned to a life of dependence' and he goes on to say: 'extrapolate on a global scale and imagine the impact of unregulated drug use in developing countries with no prevention or treatment available' (Costa, 2010). The fear in each country that the poor will become addicted to drugs that they cannot afford becomes globalized, and rich countries warn of the disaster of mass addiction in poor countries. But Costa's comments fail to acknowledge the costs of prohibition and enforcement imposed on poorer countries. In the same article he asks somewhat naively why the debate on drugs has turned into a political battle. He says 'there are no ideological debates about curing cancer, so why so much politics in dealing with drug addiction?' (ibid.). No one suggests that cancer is a good thing; everyone can agree that a cancer-free world would be a wonderful achievement. But the majority of people who use drugs do so without becoming addicted and presumably take pleasure in their recreational drug use. They see addiction as a risk worth taking. Most people accept that drugs are dangerous but they do not accept prohibition is the best way of controlling them. That is the heart of the problem with drugs. Not everyone agrees that drugs are bad or wants a drug-free world.

So far the international prohibition regime still holds together – even if the consensus is weakening. The Conventions survive partly because there is no consensus about any alternative and partly because they are sufficiently flexible to allow for some legal leeway in prohibition practice. A signatory country is required to ensure that drug possession is a criminal, not a civil offence, but this is only 'subject to its constitutional principles and the basic concepts of its legal system'. It is this loophole that has allowed some countries to treat drug possession as a civil matter. In Argentina in 2009, for example, the Supreme Court of Justice declared punishment for possession of cannabis for personal use, unconstitutional. Arand Grover, UN Special Rapporteur on the Right of Everyone to the Highest Attainable Standard of Physical and Mental Health, points out that the primary goal of the international drug control regime, as set forth in the preamble to the Single Convention on Narcotic Drugs (1961), is the 'health and welfare of mankind', but that the current approach of controlling drug use and possession works against that aim. The adverse unintended consequences of prohibition on the health and security of individuals and societies have been widely acknowledged. He argues that this entitles the UN agencies and Member States to adopt a right to health approach to drug control (Grover, 2010).

The days of drug prohibition are not yet over but it is difficult to believe they are not numbered. Discontent about prohibition is growing, but is there any evidence of a new paradigm emerging to replace it? According to Peter Hakim, 'a central roadblock to drug policy reform is the silent tolerance of ineffective, ever socially damaging, laws and policies because no specific alternative strategy has yet gathered much public support' (Hakim, 2011). Kathy Gyngell and Neil McKeganey claim that 'drug decriminalization has become the new orthodoxy' (Gyngell and McKeganey, 2011). Under the banner of harm minimization, a more flexible approach does already seem to have crept in. Antonio Maria Costa, when he was still Chief Executive of the UNODC, identified the displacement of drug policy from health to enforcement as one of the undesirable consequences of prohibition. He acknowledged the need for a greater emphasis to be place on treatment rather than imprisonment of drug users (Costa, 2008 and 2009). This shift in emphasis has been endorsed by his replacement Yury Fedotov. When he took office in September 2010 Fedotov asserted that 'drug use is a health problem, not a crime, drug users are affected by a disease, addiction, and instead of punishment, what they need is treatment, care and social integration. He emphasized the need for drug policy to encompass public health and human rights (Fedotov, 2010).

The rhetoric of the drug war has become more muted. The language has become that of harm reduction and human rights. This change in discourse may signal the emergence of a new consensus and indicate that we are now changing a climate of opinion about drugs and drug use that has been constructed over the last hundred years to support international prohibition. But this new emphasis leaves many questions unanswered. Whose harm is to be reduced? Harm to the addict and harm to society may not coincide. Harm for the addict remains the unpredictable quality and potency of their drugs, exposure to systemic crime, and in some cases insufficient access to treatment not just for substance use but treatment for pre-existing psychiatric problems or still existent problems of social deprivation, joblessness and no prospects or hope. Harm for society is high crime rates, degeneration of social spaces, and the personal insecurity this gives rise to, as well as having to foot the tax bill for whatever drug policy is in place. When we turn to human rights, again it has to be asked, whose human rights? Is it the rights of drug users and addicts who are out of step with those around them? It has already been noted (chapter 5) that in some countries, despite the shift in emphasis in the West, addicts are treated inhumanely and have no rights at all. Is it the human rights of those living in 'producer' countries, the peasants whose rights are violated by all sides, by the traffickers, the drug cartels, terrorists, paramilitaries and the government's eradication teams licensed to destroy the livelihood of the peasant farmers and are willing to resort to violence and atrocities to do so? Then there are the human rights of those who have the bad luck to live on the drug war's front line; those Mexicans caught in the crossfire of the turf wars waged by the drug cartels battling it out over market share. There may indeed be a new consensus forming around harm reduction and human rights that will satisfy well-meaning liberals. But not all drug users are addicts and not all users, or even all addicts, want treatment. Human rights provide a deceptively simply rallying call that conceals a much more complex set of claims and values.

If there is indeed a new consensus emerging, perhaps the drug warriors are right to warn that it will lead to legalization. Perhaps incrementalism is the new consensus. A hundred years ago international drug prohibition began when a small number of powerful countries agreed to prohibit the recreational use of opiates and coca-based drugs. The climate of opinion moved in favour of prohibition and it was gradually extended to include more drugs, more aspects of their cultivation, manufacture, trade and use, and more countries signed up to enforce it. Perhaps we are witnessing a reversal of that process. A few countries are beginning to break ranks. They have decriminalized drug use. Some countries are flirting with the idea of legalizing cannabis. Policy failure is prompting all but the diehard prohibitionists to rethink their positions.

The problem is measures such as the decriminalization of drugs for personal use can only be sustained if policy makers are willing to tolerate half-measures and perform a policy sleight of hand. The Dutch case demonstrates that liberalization is possible, but it is only a half-measure full of inconsistencies. One of the key arguments against prohibition is not only that it is a costly failure, but also that is does not solve the health problems surrounding the drugs themselves. Under a decriminalization regime a drug user may be freed from the fear of prosecution, and can obtain sterile injecting equipment, but what about the drugs themselves? These remain unregulated. They continue to be of unpredictable strength and unknown purity and thus continue to expose users to the dangers of overdose and those who inject and ingest drugs to the hazards of adulterated deals. In the UK, for example, the National Office of Statistics reported that the number of drug-related deaths involving heroin and morphine has risen five times since 1993 and that more than four in five of these were accidental overdoses (NOS, 2010). Decriminalization of personal use still leaves the supply of drugs in the hands of ruthless criminals with all the attendant violence of turf wars and contract enforcement. It is hard not to agree that 'drug manu-facturing and distribution is too dangerous to remain in the hands of unregulated criminals' (Moskos and Franklin, 2009). The problem with the Dutch model in respect of cannabis and those adopted in Portugal and other countries, who have decriminalized all drugs for personal use, is that supply remains fully criminalized and just as dangerous as ever. (Although, as stated earlier, the Dutch do allow cannabis users to grow up to five cannabis plants for their own use.) Caroline Lucas MP sums up the current system of drug prohibition as a 'free-for-all with no controls on who sells drugs, no controls on who can buy them, and no controls on their make-up. Every drug supplier is by definition, unlicensed, placing them beyond any form of state control or management' (Lucas, 2010).

Legalization need not mean a drug 'free-for-all'. Advocates of legalization usually add the caveat that the supply of drugs would have to be regulated. Transform, the British drug legalization pressure group, claims to have overcome the stumbling block in the debate about drug legalization: how would it work in practice? They offer the following blueprint:

1. *Medical prescription model or supervised venues* – for high-risk drugs (injecting drugs including heroin and more potent stimulants such as methamphetamine) and problematic users.
2. *Specialist pharmacist retail model* – with named/licensed user access and rationing of volume of sales for moderate-risk drugs such as amphetamine, cocaine powder and ecstasy.
3. *Licensed retailing* – including tiers of regulation appropriate to product risk and local needs. Used for lower-risk drugs and preparations such as lower-strength stimulant-based drinks.
4. *Licensed premises for sale and consumption* – similar to licensed alcohol venues and Dutch cannabis 'coffee shops', potentially also for smoking opium or poppy tea.
5. *Unlicensed sales* – minimal regulation for the least risky products, such as caffeine drinks and coca tea. (Rolles, 2010)

This model, however, is complex and it barely recognizes that most drug users are not addicts but recreational users who experience few problems with their drug use and whose drug use has little, if any adverse impact on society. Section 1 of the blueprint would mean presumably that addicts would receive prescriptions from a doctor and may even be required to use their heroin under supervision in a pharmacy. This system already exists for some long-term addicts. But it faces the perennial problem of who determines which users come into the category of being allowed prescription heroin, and it would presumably leave many users outside still scoring street heroin. Section 5 seems to imply regulation where at present no regulation exists for the psychoactive substances in this category. Models of regulation, other than something resembling those used for alcohol and tobacco, medicalize drug use, by making the medical profession the guardians of access, and are likely to perpetuate the stereotypes of the marginalized and stigmatized junkie. We do not separate different kinds of alcoholic drinkers and insist that those who drink spirits or who have had an alcohol problem can only get their alcohol from a pharmacy.

Transform acknowledges that legalization and regulation might have to be introduced piecemeal and cautiously and be closely monitored and evaluated for any unintended negative consequences (Rolles, 2010). It also admits that regulation is 'no silver bullet and that in the short term it can only seek to reduce the problems that stem from prohibition and the illicit trade it has created' (Rolles, 2010). But this still leaves a lot of devil in the detail of how legalization of supply would be managed. The alcohol industry is circumscribed by regulation. Alcoholic drink is tested for its alcohol content, the measures in which it is sold are controlled and subject to regular checks, licensing hours are a matter for the law, as is the age at which people are legally allowed to drink. On top of these details, there are also questions about how the supply of currently illegal drugs would be actually come about. Would the current drug-rich criminals be persuaded to become legitimate and accept lower profits? Would there be a stampede of suppliers of legal recreational drugs to get in on this currently illegal and lucrative trade? Would the pharmaceutical companies muscle into the supply of the previously prohibited range of drugs?

Drugs cause many problems, but prohibition causes many more. Legalization would only solve some of the problems caused by prohibition. Criminals and terrorists would still seek profits and they would most likely shift the focus of their activities more towards robbery, armaments, people smuggling, vice and kidnapping. There would still be street gangs fighting over turf and committing crimes. Legalization would not stop crime, but it would stop us from punishing young people all over the world and exposing them to the criminals who control drug supply and criminals with whom they may end up sharing a prison cell. No doubt drug users would no longer be exposed to the health dangers of adulterated drugs of unknown strength, and most addicts would be able to obtain a cheaper, cleaner deal that may help them resist economic compulsive crime, but there would still be drug addicts with health problems themselves, and who cause problems for their families, and in the rich countries, the taxpayers.

Would legalization unleash a drug epidemic of unimaginable proportions? No one can know. It might, but then not everyone who drinks becomes an obnoxious drunk or an alcoholic. Most people who want to use drugs have no difficulty in obtaining them now, but they do run the additional health hazards and risks of prosecution that prohibition entails. Prohibition has failed to fix the drug problem. Legalization will fix some of the problems caused by prohibition, but there will still be a drug problem just as there is an alcohol problem. However, drugs would cease to be a problem of criminal justice and eventually become just a medical and social problem as is the case with alcohol.

8
Conclusion

There is an uncomfortable similarity between the drug addict and those who support drug prohibition. The addict comes to see a fix as the solution to life's problems, the prohibitionists have come to see prohibition as the fix for drug problems which are also part of life itself.

Nobody sets out to be a drug addict. Daring, boredom, desperation, curiosity, expectation of pleasure, peer group pressure, seeking to solve problems, self-medication, any or several of these help to explain why someone might try a drug like heroin. Satisfaction of some or several of these impulses may explain continued use. All too soon the user who started out in control of their drug consumption can become the addict controlled by the drug. Relationships, money, integrity, health and home are often sacrificed to the drug. The addict may deal, steal or prostitute themselves for a fix. A chaotic, driven lifestyle is the result. Friends and family may beg the addict to do something, to seek help, but the addict often fails to recognize that they have a problem, or if they have a problem it is not with the drug. Those who treat addiction describe this as being in a state of denial. The addict may lose their family and friends. They may be in and out of prison, they might suffer serious health problems, and they may be cheated and beaten up by dealers and robbed by other addicts. They may be coerced into treatment, but in the end it is only when they acknowledge that their drug use is a problem, even *the* problem, that they can do anything about their addiction.

Governments see drug use as problematical. They fear that if the number of addicts become numerous then the result might be the destruction of states and societies as we know them. Seeking a solution to this governments settle on the prohibition of some psychoactive drugs and the regulation of others. It seemed like a good idea. Once one or two countries were persuaded prohibition was a good idea, they then put peer pressure on other countries to join an international prohibition regime, under the auspices of the United Nations.

But prohibiting desire simply does not work. Prohibition has to be enforced. Supply has to be eradicated, or interdicted, producers, traffickers, dealers, those caught in possession of drugs and in some countries, users of drugs, have to be punished. Liberties are lost, human rights are violated, and corruption and violence become common-place, health problems increase and trillions of taxpayers' dollars are sacrificed to feed the prohibition fix.

Critical friends begin to ask whether this solution is worse than the original problem, which was in any case partly fear of a potential problem only. But it is the prohibitionists who are in denial and the anti-drug industry cannot imagine a world without the fight against drugs. They advocate more of the same: greater enforcement and increasingly severe penalties. They are either unable to acknowledge all of the difficulties and waste that prohibition itself has caused, or, because of their deeply held belief that drugs are evil, see the difficulties caused by prohibition as just unfortunate collateral damage. But prohibitionists will not change unless they can accept that just as the 'drugs don't work' as a cure for the addict's life problems, prohibition does not solve society's problems with drugs. In the end, just as drugs make the addict's life a misery, prohibition has the potential to make everyone's life a misery. Johann Hari described proponents of the war on drugs as 'well-intentioned people who believe they are saving people from the nightmare of drug addiction and making the world safer. But this self-image has turned into a faith – and like all faiths it can only be maintained by cultivating deliberate blindness to the evidence' (Hari, 2009).

Just as drug users vary, so, as we have noted, do prohibitionists. For the diehard anti-drugs lobby prohibition is a matter of faith. Drugs are wicked; only by banning them can the world and individuals be saved from the corruption of drugs. Prohibition is *the* fix. But Johann Hari is wrong in claiming that prohibition is a matter of faith for all who have and do support it. There are those who accept prohibition as a practical response to a practical problem. Drugs can and do destroy individuals and families and have the potential for destroying the wider society, and even if the crime and corruption can be blamed on prohibition, there would still be the drain on the public purse of supporting and treating addicts. This group do not necessarily believe that every user will become an addict, but they do believe that widespread drug addiction would be a huge practical problem that conceivably could undermine the stability of states and societies. For this latter group prohibition is *a* fix but one that is contingent upon it working, that is, solving the problem.

Are policy makers still in denial or are they now able to accept the evidence that prohibition has not only failed to solve the drug problem but has actually made the situation much worse? It is difficult to be sure when any addict has reached a turning point. Some simply cannot accept that the drug no longer solves their problems and even the thought of withdrawal symptoms causes panic, anxiety and a craving for a fix. The diehard drug warriors will never accept that prohibition has failed. They cling to the belief that it is a lack of political will to enforce prohibition properly that is at the root of its apparent failure. They may be right. It is indeed possible to look at cases where prohibition appears to have been successfully enforced backed by strong political determination. According to Booth, 'after the Communist Revolution in China opium stocks were publicly burned, deviants were destroyed; dealers were either killed or sent for "political re-education" in labour camps. Poppy fields were burnt. Pipes were publicly destroyed. Opium taking was listed officially as unhealthy, anti-social, anti-socialist and a capitalist activity' (Booth, 1998, 168–9). Dikötter says much the same. He describes how, after the Chinese Communist Party took over the government of China in 1949, it took the party 'a mere three years to radically eliminate all illegal substances: a dense network of police institutions, resident committees and mass organizations were used to crush drug offenders ... public trials and mass executions dealt the final blow to the narcotic culture' (Dikötter, 2004, 208). Although prohibition as we know it has eroded some aspect of a free society, it has not reached the extremes described by Booth and by Dikӧotter and seems unlikely ever to do so in liberal democracies. Dikötter does go on to say that although the ruthless enforcement of prohibition did seem to wipe out visible drug use, enforcement benefited from a pre-existing shift in the drug culture that could be identified by the 1930s in China. The social status of opium had begun to decline and abstinence came to be seen as a mark of pride and sign of modernity among social elites (ibid.). This in turn was reinforced in the 1940s when penicillin became available for the treatment of a whole range of diseases for which people had previously self-medicated with opium. Ruthless enforcement did work but it was not the only explanation for the decline in the Chinese opium habit.

Looking at the history of drug control through a longer lens than that of the twentieth century teaches us that drugs that are initially regarded as alien and outlawed often eventually become assimilated into the culture. They may be rejected at first and then be fully accepted, as happened in the case of coffee, or they may be prohibited, as in the case of tobacco, eventually gain acceptance and subsequently, as more becomes known about the harms it may cause, remained legal but the habit of smoking has become much less socially accepted and more tightly regulated, in the West anyway.

Authorities' fear of drugs is shaped not by what is but by what might be. It is the fear that if drugs were legalized a heroin republic would be the result. This would be a state in which the number of non-productive, feckless drugs users outnumbers those who eschew drugs and keep the wheels of work turning, pay their taxes and underwrite everybody's welfare bill. But this spectre has more to do with prohibition than drugs themselves. First it assumes that if drugs were legal everyone would try them and many, if not the majority, would become addicted. Yet we know already that for many people using drugs is a temporary, youthful transgression. Second we know that most people who use illegal drugs do so with little harm to themselves or society. They use them recreationally. They may smoke cannabis to relax at home, or take ecstasy or snort a few lines of cocaine when they go out partying, in just the same way as the non-problem drinker may have a beer or glass or wine to help them to relax or to improve a social occasion. The drug problem is not drugs themselves but drug users for whom drug use changes from occasional and recreational use to compulsive use, and much of what is commonly regarded as the drug problem, crime and corruption, is in fact a problem stemming from prohibition. Because drugs are illegal this kind of user is forced to pay a premium black market price for drugs of unknown purity, unpredictable strength and unreliable availability. If the drugs to which they are addicted were legal some of these kinds of problems would no longer plague us. Secondly, a growing body of evidence on the usefulness of Heroin Assisted Treatment suggests that heroin addicts who have access to a regular and pure source of their drug can lead normal, useful lives (there will, of course, always be some exceptions, such as people for whom drug use is self-medication for other pre-existing conditions). Our fears of the heroin republic were largely shaped by the tales of the missionaries to China who depicted a society almost completely depraved and corrupted by opium. The USA took up the cause and initiated what has become a hundred-year crusade against, certain but not all, psychoactive drugs. China provided a model of what a drug dystopia might be like that prompted a clamour for prohibition, but it need not have been the model. In the first place, the model China provided may have been misconstrued and the opium plague of the nineteenth century may have been exaggerated. In a country with no antibiotics or aspirin, opium was a 'cure all'. Secondly, there was another model which could have shaped our views on drugs, particularly the American view. In 1782 J. Hector St John Crevecoeur, a French aristocrat married to an American, published his collection of 'Letters from an American Farmer'. These letters describe what he discovered about people in the New World. Letter VIII is of particular interest here. In it he describes 'the peculiar customs at Nantucket'. He tells us how these Puritan fishing communities celebrate hard work and disapprove of inebriation. He notes that the men are often away at sea for long periods and that in their absence the women are highly organized and industrious. But he then goes on to tell us how surprised he is to discover 'a singular custom that prevails here among the women' and that he is at a loss to explain how it has been introduced in this primitive society:

> They have adopted these many years, the Asiatic custom of taking a dose of opium every morning; and so deeply rooted is it, that they would be at a loss how to iive without this indulgence; they would rather be deprived of any necessity than forego their favourite luxury. This is much more prevailing among the women than the men, few of the latter having caught the contagion; though the sheriff, whom I may call the first person in the island, who is an eminent physician besides, ... has for many years submitted to

this custom. He takes three grains of it every day after breakfast, without the effects of which, he often told me, he was not able to transact any business. (Crevecoeur, 1782)

Crevecoeur's account suggests that drug use, even addiction, and being a useful member of society are not necessarily mutually exclusive.

The arguments for legalizing all drugs are certainly intellectually compelling but practically less so. Angus McQueen argues that 'drug policies have little to do with science, health or harm. They have been hijacked by the emotive rhetoric of moralists' (McQueen, 2010). This is not quite right. There is indeed a great deal of anti-drug rhetoric and misunderstanding, but drugs do cause harm. Drug use, legal or illegal, will always cause some people to become addicted and some people to inflict harm on others. Families break up, children are abused and some peoples' drug use will lead to financial ruin and perhaps intentional overdose. Problem drug users will still need treatment; they may be unemployed and have to live on benefits, so they will continue to be both a social and economic cost to society. Recognizing that prohibition has failed to solve these problems and has actually caused more problems, is not the same as claiming that drugs are not problematical.

This book began with the claim that the drug problem is complex and unsolvable. One hundred years ago prohibition became the favoured solution, but it has solved nothing, cost a fortune, exacerbated the existing drug problems and brought with it a whole range of negative side effects. Criminals and insurgents have benefited from the prohibition dividend. Taxpayers have funded a job creation scheme for providers of security, prisons, lawyers and all kinds of bureaucrats. But the caution that the drug problem is unsolvable also applies to decriminalization, legalization and regulation. Dismissing all the alternatives, James Brokenshire, the current minister with responsibility for drugs policy at the British Home Office, said

decriminalisation is a simplistic solution that fails to recognize the complexity of the problem and ignores the serious harm drug-taking poses to the individual. Legalization fails to address the reasons people misuse drugs in the first place or the misery, cost and lost opportunities that dependence causes individuals, their families and the wider community. (Brokenshire, 2010)

He is correct in describing the problem as complex and warning against 'simplistic' solutions. But prohibition itself is a simplistic solution, which practice has shown to be no solution at all. Each of these proposed solutions may bring some improvements, and certainly the trend towards the decriminalization of possession helps to shift the problem of drugs from the sphere of criminal justice in the direction of the public health model, but each may also bring further problems. Decriminalization of possession solves the problem of young people who use drugs acquiring criminal records, it would reduce some of the costs of criminal justice, but it leaves the question of supply unanswered. It is simply impossible to estimate the extent to which prohibition has deterred wider use of drugs or to predict the extent to which drug use, and therefore the number of problem drug users, might increase if drugs were legal. The drug problem is perennial. People want to use psychoactive substances, but these substances have both positive and negative outcomes for individuals and societies. This is a problem to be managed rather than solved.

Prohibition is no longer the least-worst option and legalization and regulation may offer a least-worse option for the future. The fix that the drug user and the addict seek does not solve the complex problems thrown up by life and brings only temporary pleasure or respite. Society's problems with drugs are complex, but permanent. Prohibition is fixable, drugs are not.

Bibliography

Abrams, Elliot (1986) 'Drug War: The New Alliance Against Traffickers and Terrorists'. Speech before the Council of Foreign Relations in New York, 10 February 1986. Published as Current Policy No. 792 US Dept State Bureau of Public Affairs.

Abramsky, Sasha (2009) 'Sign of High Times'. *Guardian*, 21 October.

Ainsworth, Bob (2010) Drug Policy Debate, 16 December. www.parliament.uk.

Anslinger, Harry J. (1937) Hearings House of Representatives Ways and Means Committee 1937.

Allen-Mills, Tony (2010a) 'Mexican Drug Gangs Worship Saint Death', *Sunday Times*, 15 March.

Allen-Mills, Tony (2010b) 'Drug Wars Shatter Pearl of the Pacific', *Sunday Times*, 3 October.

Arbabzadah, Nushin (2010) 'Killer Fungus is No Mystery to Afghan Poppy Growers', *Guardian*, 17 May.

Ayling, Julie (2005) 'Conscription in the War on Drugs: Recent Reforms to the US Drug Certification Process', *International Journal of Drug Policy*, 16.

Bale, David (2008) 'Drug Addict Asks to Go to Jail', *Evening News (Norwich)*, 22 February.

Bancroft, Angus (2009) *Drugs, Intoxication and Society* (Polity).

Bannerman, Lucy and O'Neill, Sean (2010) 'Millionaire Drug Dealer Jailed But Britain's Cocaine Explosion Goes On', *The Times*, 5 March.

Barbor, T. et al. (2010) *Drug Policy and the Public Good* (Oxford University Press).

Barret, Damon, Lines, Rich, Schleifer, Rebecca and Bewley-Taylor, Dave (2009) 'Recalibrating the Regime: The Need for a Human Rights-Based Approach to International Drug Policy', Beckley Foundation Report 13 (Beckley Foundation.

BBC News (1999) 'Business: The Company File: The Economics of Tobacco', 28 September.

BBC News (2009) 'Skunk Bigger Psychosis Risk Than Other Cannabis Types', 1 December.

BBC News (2010a) 14 July.

BBC News (2010b) 4 August.

Bean, Philip (1974) *The Social Control of Drugs* (Martin Robertson).

Bean, Philip and Nemtze, Teresa (2004) *Drug Treatment: What Works?* (Routledge).

Bean, Philip and Whynes, David (eds) (1991) *Policing and Prescribing* (Macmillan).

Becker, H. (1967) 'History, Culture and Subjective Experience: an Exploration of the Social Basis of Drug-Induced Experiences', *Journal of Health and Social Behaviour*, 8(3), 163–76.

Bentham, Mandy (1998) *The Politics of Drug Control* (Palgrave).

Blackman, Shane (2004) *Chilling Out* (Open University Press).

Blakemore, Colin (2010) 'Our Crusade Against Chemistry Has Failed', *The Times*, 24 August.

Benavie, Arthur (2009) *Drugs: America's Holy War* (Routledge).

Bennett, Trevor and Holloway, Katy (2007) *Drug-Crime Connections* (Cambridge).

Berger, Judson (2009) 'What's in a Name? Re-branding Madness Consumes Washington', *Fox News*, 18 May.

Berger, Sebastien (2005) 'Asparagus is Winning Battle Against Opium', *Telegraph*, 4 March.

Berridge, Virginia (1991) 'AIDS and British Drug Policy: History Repeats Itself', in Philip Bean and David Whynes (eds), *Policing and Prescribing* (Macmillan).

Bewley-Taylor, Dave (1999) *The United States and International Drug Control 1909–1997* (Pinter).

Bewley-Taylor, Dave, Hallam, Chris and Allen, Rob (2009) 'The Incarceration of Drug Offenders' (Beckley Foundation).

Beyer, Chris (2010) 'Detention as Treatment' (Open Society Institute).

Bickman, Tom and Jelsma, Martin (2009) 'Drug Policy Reform in Practice' (TNI).

Birdwill, Jonathan, Chapman, Jake and Singleton, Nicola (2011) 'Taking Drugs Seriously' (Demos and UKDPC).

Booth, M. (1998) *Opium: A History* (St Martin's Press).

Booth, William (2010) 'Mexico Hobbled in Drug War by Arrests that Lead Nowhere', *Washington Post*, 26 April.

Bowers, Simon (2011) 'Heroin Treatment Boosts Reckitt Profits', *Guardian* 20 April.

Bowling, Ben (2010) 'Jamaica Bleeds for Our "War on Drugs"', *Guardian* 27 May.

Brailsford, Guy (1989) 'Opium Crop Substitution Programme Achi District Nangarhar', http://pdf.usaid./gove/pdf_docs/PCAAA970.pdf.

Brewer, Colin (2008) 'Social and Economic Benefits of Ending the "War on Drugs"', in Patricia Cholweka, and Mitra Motlagh (eds), *Health Capital and Sustainable Socioeconomic Development* (Harwood).

British Crime Survey (2009) (Home Office). Available online at homeoffice.gov.uk.

Brokenshire, James (2010) cit Humphreys, John yougov.co.uk/commentaries/john-humphreys/war-drugs-time-admit-defeat, 21 December.

Brown, Mev (2010) 'Why Waging a War on Drugs is Futile', *Scotsman*, 4 October.

Bullington, Bruce (1998) 'America's Drug War: Fact or Fiction?', in Ross Coomber (ed.), *The Control of Drugs and Drug Users* (CRC Press).

Burke, Jason (2004) 'Creation of an Opium Giant', *Druglink* Nov./Dec.

Buxton, Julia (2006) *The Political Economy of Narcotics* (Zed Books).

Campbell, Denis (2009) 'Cocaine Drug of Choice for Under-25s', *Guardian*, 4 October.

Campbell, Duncan (2002) 'Bush tars drug-takers with aiding terrorists', Guardian, 8 August.

Carnworth, Tim and Smith, Ian (2002) *Heroin Century* (Routledge).

Carrell, Severin (2010) 'Anthrax-contaminated Heroin Kills Drug Users', *Guardian*, 10 February.

Cavendish, Camilla (2006) 'The War on Drugs is Not the War on Terror', *The Times*, 8 June.

Chaiken, J. and Chaiken, M. (1990) 'Drugs and Predatory Crime', in M. Tonry and J.Q. Wilson (eds), *Drugs and Crime: Criminal Justice* (Chicago University Press).

Chouvy, Pierre-Arnaud (2002) 'Drugs and War Destabilize Thai–Myanmar Border Region', *Jane's Intelligence Review*, 1 April.

Clawson, Patrick and Lee III, Rensselaer (1998) *The Andean Cocaine Industry* (Macmillan).

CNN (2009) 'Pregnant and Addicted: Mothers in South Carolina Find Hope', 23 October.

Cockburn, Alexander and St Clair, Jeffrey (1998) *Whiteout: The CIA, Drugs and the Press* (Verso).

Coelho, Manuel Pinto (2010) 'Portugal's Drug Policy is a Poor Model for Our Own' (letter), *Observer*, 19 September.

Collins, James J (1990) 'Summary Thoughts about Drugs and Violence', in Ross Coomber (ed.), *Drugs and Drug Use in Society* (Greenwich University Press).

Collison M (1996) 'In Search of the High Life: Drugs, Crime, Masculinities and Consumption', *British Journal of Criminology*, 36(3), 428–43.

Coomber, Ross and South, Nigel (2004) *Drug Use and Culture* (Free Association Books).

Corbin, Jane (2005) 'Britain's Heroin Fix', BBC *Panorama*, 24 July.

Costa, Antonio Maria (2008) 'Making Drug Control Fit for Purpose: Building on UNGASS Decade', *Daily Mail*, 18 April.

Costa, Antonio Maria (2009) 'How Many Lives Would Have Been Lost if We Didn't Have Controls on Drugs?', *Guardian*, 20 September.

Costa, Antonio Maria (2010) 'Legalize Drugs and a Worldwide Epidemic of Addiction Will Follow', *Observer*, 5 September.

Courtwright, David (2001) *Forces of Habit* (Harvard University Press).

Crandall, Russell (2008) *Driven by Drugs*, 2nd edn (Lynne Reinner).

Crevecoeur, J Hector St John 1782 *Letters from an American Farmer*, http://xroads.virginia.edu/~hyper/CREV/home.html.

Dalrymple, Theodore (2007) *Junk Medicine: Doctors, Lies and the Addiction Bureaucracy* (Harriman House).

Daly, Max (2007) 'Fishing with Dogs', *Druglink*, Nov./Dec.

Davenport-Hines, Richard (2002) *The Pursuit of Oblivion* (Phoenix).

Department of Health (2009) www.dh.gov.uk/News/Recentstories/dh_100607.

Dellios, Hugh (2006) 'Mexico Backs off Legalizing Drug Use', *Seattle Times*, 4 May.

Dikötter, F., Laamann L. and Xun, Zhou (2004) *Narcotic Culture* (Hurst).

Dillon, Patrick, (2002) 'Out of Addiction's Grip', *Sunday Times*, 2 June.

Donegan, Lawrence (2002) 'US Pupils Face Random Drug Testing', *Observer*, 2 June.

Dorn, Nigel (1981) 'Social Analyses of Drugs in Health Education and Media', in Griffith Edwards and Carol Brusch (eds), *Drug Problems in Britain* (Academic Press).

Doyle, Jack (2011) 'Luvvies for Legalisation: You're Being Naïve in the Extreme, Celebrities Told after Drugs Plea to PM', *Mail OnLine*, 3 June.

Druglink (2010) March/April.

Duke, Steven B and Gross, Albert (1982) *America's Longest War* (Putnam and Sons).

Dunt, Ian (2010) 'Experts Turn Against War on Drugs', www.politics.co.uk, 23 July.

Dutch News.nl (2010) 'Let Cannabis Cafes Grow Their Own Weed, Says Mayor', 10 November.

Dwyer, Jim 2009 'Whites Smoke Pot, but Blacks Are Arrested', *New York Times*, 22 December.

Economist (2009) 'Why a Tight Market for Drugs May be Contributing to Violence', 22 October.

Economist (2010) 'A Toker's Guide', 5 March.

Edwards, Griffith (2004) *A Matter of Substance* (Allen Lane).

Engel, Matthew (2009) 'Why It's Time to End the War on Drugs', *Financial Times*, 31 July.

European Monitoring Centre for Drugs and Drug Addiction (2011) *Annual Report* (European Monitoring Centre for Drugs and Drug Addiction).

Faggiano, F., Vigna-Taglianti, F., Burkhart, G. et al. (2010) 'Effectiveness of a School-based Substance Abuse Prevention Program', *Drug and Alcohol Dependence*, 108.

Farthing, Linda (1997) 'Social Impacts Associated with Ant-Drug Act 1008', in M.B. Leons and H. Sanabria (eds), *Coca, Cocaine and the Bolivian Reality* (Reading University Press).

Fazey, Cindy (2003) 'Commission on Narcotic Drugs and the United Nations International Drug Control Programme: Politics, Policies and Prospects for Change', *International Journal of Drug Policy*, 14, 2 April.

Federal Drug Control Programs (2003) www.gpoaccess.gov/usbudget/fy03/pdf/bud32.pdf.

Fedotov, Yuri (2010) www.UNODC, 29 November.

Felbab-Brown, Vanda *Shooting-Up: Counterinsurgency and the War on Drugs* (Brookings Institute).

Fielding, Tom (2009) *The Candy Machine: How Cocaine Took Over the World* (Penguin).

Findings (2011) 'Effectiveness of a School-based Substance Abuse Prevention Programme', http://findings.org.uk/count/downloads/download.php?file=Fagianno_F_9.txt.

Fitzgerald, Scott (2010) 'Drug-addicted Mom Abuses Child by Breastfeeding', NBC Miami, 23 September.

Ford, Richard (2010a) 'Celebrity Users Made Cocaine All the Rage, say MPs', *The Times*, 3 March.

Ford, Richard (2010b) 'Illegal Drug Trade is Thriving Despite a Battle That Costs Britain Billions', *The Times*, 24 August.

Flynn, Paul (2009) *Drink and Drugs News*, 27 July.

Freeman, Laurie and Sierra, Jorge Louis (2005) 'Mexico: The Militarization of Drug Policy', in Coletta Youngers and Eileen Rosin (eds), *Drugs and Democracy in Latin America* (Lynne Reinner).

Friedman, Milton (1990) Letter to Bill Bennet, reproduced in Rod L. Evans and Irwin M. Berent (eds), *Drug Legalization: For and Against* (Open Court Publishing, 1992).

Gabbat, Adam (2011) 'Medical Marijuana Superstore Opens in Arizona', *Guardian*, 2 June.

Galen-Carpenter, Ted (2003) *Bad Neighbour Policy* (Palgrave).

Galen-Carpenter, Ted (2005) 'Mexico is Become the Next Colombia' (TNI).

Galluhue, Patrick (2010) 'A Worrying Front in the War on Drugs', *Guardian*, 6 June.

Gamina, Gabriella (2001) 'Drug Smugglers Dig Tunnels in US', *The Times*, 8 March.

Glenny, Misha (2009) 'Drugs Cartels Open Another Front in a Futile War', *Financial Times*, 10 December.

Global Commision on Drug Policy (2011) *Report*. Accessed at http://www.globalcommissionondrugs.org/Report.

Goldberg, Suzanne (2010) 'George Soros Gives $1 Million to California's Pro-cannabis Campaign', *Guardian*, 26 October.

Goldstein, P.J. (1985) 'The Drugs–Violence Nexus: A Tripartite Conceptual Framework', *Journal of Drug Issues*, 15, 493–506.

Goodman, Jordan, Lovejoy, Paul E and Sherrat, Andrew (eds) (2007) *Consuming Habits*, 2nd edn (Routledge).

Goodsir, Jane (1993) 'Civil Rights and Civil Liberties Surrounding the Use of Cocaine and Crack', in Bean, Philip (ed.), *Cocaine and Crack Supply and Use* (Macmillan).

Grantham Journal (2010) 'Addict Mum pleads "Lock Me Up for Christmas"', 17 December.

Gray, John (2009) 'The Case for Legalising All Drugs is Unanswerable?', *Observer*, 13 September.

Greaves, Mike (2000) Britain's Secret War on Drugs', BBC *Panorama*, 2 October.

Greater Manchester Police (2010) www.gmp.police.uk, 11 February.

Greenwald, Glenn (2009) 'Drug Decriminalization in Portugal', CATO Institute, 2.

Grover, Arand (2010) www.ungassondrugs.org.

Guardian (no by-line) (2010) 'Mexico Drug War – As Violence Spirals So Does Spending on Security', 13 October.

Gutling, Stephen (2009) 'The Racism of Marijuana Prohibition', *Los Angeles Times*.

Gyngell, Kathy (2009) 'Whatever Happened to the NTA's "Emperor's New Clothes" Movement?' www.cps.org.uk.

Gyngell, Kathy (2010) Cited in *The Times*, 24 August.

Gyngell, Kathy and McKeganey, Neil (2011) 'Drug Decriminalization – The New Orthodoxy', www.cps.org.uk, 9 May.

Hakim, Peter (2011) 'Rethinking US Drug Policy: Inter-American Dialogue' (Beckley Foundation).

Hall, Wayne and Degenhardt, Louisa (2011) 'Cannabis and the Increased Incidence and Persistence of Psychosis', *British Medical Journal*, 4 March.

Hallam, Christopher (2010a) '"Jar Wars": The Question of Schools-based Drug Testing', April (IDPC).

Hallam, Christopher (2010b) 'Heroin Assisted Treatment', Briefing Paper (IPDC).

Hammersley, Richard (2008) *Drugs and Crime* (Polity).

Hari, Johann (2009) 'Accept the Fact – and End this Futile "War on Drugs"', *Independent*, 11 November.

Harris, John (2009) 'Westminster's Drugs Paranoia Can't Last', *Guardian*, 2 November.

Harris, John (2011) 'The Alcohol and the Ecstasy: Prejudice Drowns Out Sense', *Guardian*, 21 February.

Harris, Paul (2010) 'Prop 19 to Legalise Marijuana Defeated in California', *Guardian*, 3 November.

Hartnoll, Richard (1998) 'International Trends', in Coomber, Ross (ed.), *Control of Drugs and Drug Users* (Harwood Academic).

Harvey, Mike (2009) 'California Dreaming of Full Marijuana Legalisation', *Time*, 28 September.

Hawley, Chris (2010) 'Drug Cartels Threaten Mexican Stability', *USA Today*, 10 February.

Hays, Paul (2010) 'New Figures Show Drug Treatment is Value for Money', National Treatment Agency (NTA), 4 March, www.nta.nhs.uk.

Haynes, Andrew (2010) 'The Animal World Has Junkies Too', *Pharmacy Journal* on line 285: 723.

Heffer, Simon (2010) 'Get Tough on Drugs, Don't Legalise Them', *Telegraph*, 17 December.

Helmer, John (1977) 'The Connection Between Narcotics and Crime', *Journal of Drug Issues*, 7(4), 405–18.

Henry, Julie, Barret, David, and Ralph, Alex (2009) 'Drugs Not Harmful, Children Told by Helpline', *Sunday Telegraph*, 19 April.

Hodgson, Martin (2001) 'Colombian Farmers Count the Cost of Airborne Assault on Drug Fields', *Guardian*, 27 February.

Holder, Harold (2009) 'Prevention Programs in the Twenty-first Century: What We Do Not Discuss in Public', *Addiction Studies*, 105(4).

Home Office (2005) *Tackling Drugs: Changing Lives* (Home Office).

Homer, *The Odyssey*, 2004 edn (CRW Publishing).

Honer, G.W., Gewirtz, G. and Tuvey, M. (1987) 'Psychosis and Violence in Cocaine Smokers', *Lancet*, 2.

Hope, Christopher (2009) 'Cannabis "Can Cause Psychosis in Healthy People"', *Telegraph*, 27 July.

Human Rights Watch (2003) 'Locked Doors: The Human Rights of People With HIV/AIDS in China' (Human Rights Watch).

Hurtado, Gomez (1993) Address to The European Cities' Drug Policy Forum.

Husak, Douglas (2000) 'Liberal Neutrality, Autonomy and Drug Prohibitions', *Philosophy and Public Affairs*, 28(6).

Icasualties http://icasualties.org/oef.

Islam, Faisal (2002) 'Class A Capitalists', *Observer*, 21 April.

Jay, M. (2010) *High Society* (Wellcome Institute).

Jack, Ian (2009) 'Why Target the Poppy Fields and Not the Breweries?', *Guardian*, 12 September.

James I (1604) *Counterblaste to Tobacco* Available online at http://extra.shu.ac.uk/iemls/resour/mirrors/rbear/james1.html.

Jelsma, Martin, Kramer, Tom and Vervest, Pietje (eds) (2005) *Trouble in the Triangle: Opium and Conflict in Burma* (Silkworm Books).

Jelsma, Martin (2011) 'Lessons Learned and Strategic Challenges for the Future' (Transnational Institute).

Jenkins, Simon (2010) 'Our "War on Drugs" Has Been an Abysmal Failure, Just Look at Mexico', *Guardian*, 9 September.

Jill (2007) 'Prosecuting Pregnant Drug-addicted Mothers', http://www.Feministe.us/blog/archives/2007/05/24/prosectuting-pregnant-drug-addicted-mothers.

Johnston, Philip (2009) 'Cannabis Confusion is Labour's Fault, not Professor Nutt's', *Telegraph*, 3 November.

Kaplan, John (2003) *Heroin: The Hardest Drug* (Chicago University Press).

Keegan, Nigel (2010) 'Drug Decriminalization in Portugal', *British Medical Journal*, 5 October.

Keohane, Joseph and Nye, Robert (eds) (1971) *Transnational Relations in World Politics* (Harvard University Press).

Kirby, Terry (2009) 'Over the Limit', *Guardian*, 10 September.

Klein, Alex (2008) *Drugs and the World* (Reaktion Books).

Kleinman, Mark (2006) 'Prohibition: A Rum Do', *Druglink*, July/August.

Kristof, Nichole (2009) 'Drugs Won the War', *New York Times*, 14 June.

Lakhani, Nina (2009) 'One in 500 Babies Now Born Drug Addicted', *Independent*, 31 May.

Lart, Rachel (1998) 'Medical Power/knowledge: The Treatment and Control of Drugs and Drug Users', in Ross Coomber (ed.), *The Control of Drugs and Drugs Users* (CRC Press).

Lacey, Marc (2010) 'Despite the Killing, Mexican Backs Drug Policy', *New York Times*, 14 June.

Lee III, Rensselear (1989) *The White Labyrinth* (Transaction).

Lewis, David (2009) 'West African Cocaine Use Rises Along Smuggling Routes', *Washington Post*, 14 February.

Light, A.B. and Torrance, E.G. (1929) 'The Effect of the Abrupt Withdrawal Followed by Administration of Morphine to Heroin Addicts', *Archives of Internal Medicine*, 44.

Lister, Stuart, Seddon, Toby, Wincup, Emma, Barrett, Sam and Traynor, Peter (2008) 'Street Policing of Problem Drug Users' (Joseph Rowntree Foundation).

Livingstone, Grace (2003) *Inside Colombia: Drugs, Democracy and War* (Latin American Bureau).

Lloyd, Charlie (2010) 'Sinning and Sinned Against: The Stigmatisation of Problem Drug Users' (UKDPC).

Lloyd, Tom (2009) 'War of Drugs is a Waste of Time', *Guardian*, 21 September.

Lucas, Caroline MP (2010) Drugs Policy Debate, 16 December. www.parliament.uk.

Lusane, Clarence (1991) *Pipe Dream Blues Racism and the War on Drugs* (South End Press).

MacDonald, Stuart (2009) 'Police Seize Only 1% of Heroin', *The Times*, 21 June.

Maddox, Bronwen (2010) 'Drugs Violence in Mexico Will Focus US Attention Closer to Home' *Times* 6 March.

Makarenko, Tamara (2002) 'Crime, Terror and the Central Asian Drug Trade', *Harvard Asia Quarterly*, 6(3).

Mangold, Tom (2000) 'Britain's Secret War on Drugs', *Panorama*, BBC, 2 October.

Manning, Peter K. (2004) *Narcs' Game* (Waveland).

Manschreck, T.C., Allen, D.F. and Neville, M. (1990) 'Freebase Psychosis: Cases from a Bahamian Epidemic of Cocaine Abuse', *Comparative Psychology*, 31(4).

Mansfield, David and Sage, Colin (1989) 'Drug Crop Producing Countries: A Development Perspective', in Ross Coomber (ed.), *The Control of Drugs and Drug Users* (CRC Press).

Marks, Amber (2008) *Headspace: On the Trail of Sniffer Dogs, Wasp Wardens and Other Dumb Friends in the Surveillance Industry* (Virgin Books).

Mathers, Bradley M et al. (2008) 'Global Epidemiology of Injecting Drug Use and HIV Among People Who Injects Drugs: Systematic Review', *The Lancet*, 372, 1733–45.

McAllister, William B (2000) *Drug Diplomacy in the Twentieth Century* (Routledge).

McCoun, R. and Reuter, P. (2001) *Drug War Heresies* (Cambridge University Press).

McGinty, Stephen (2010) 'Keeping an Addict on Drugs', *Scotsman*, 29 March.

McKeganey, Neil (2005) 'Random Drug Testing in School of School Children' (Joseph Rowntree Foundation).

McKeganey, Neil (2010) 'National Treatment Agency Treatment Outcome Research: Hard Evidence or Political Spin?', *Addiction Today*. Available online at http://www.addictiontoday.org/addictiontoday/2010/10/nta-treatment-outcome-research.html.

McKie, Robin (2009) 'US Stars Are Falling Victim to Prescription Drugs', *Observer*, 27 December.

McKinley Jr, James (2010) 'Mexican Drug Kingpin Sentences to 25 Years at Secret Hearing', *New York Times*, 25 February.

McQueen, Angus (2010) 'Why Do We So Wilfully Cover Up the Failure of the War on Drugs?', *Observer*, 1 August.

Meyer, Maureen, with contributions from Brewer, Stephanie and Cepeda, Carlos (2010) 'Abused and Afraid in Ciudad Juarez – An Analysis of Human Rights Violations by the Military in Mexico' (WOLA).

Miglierini, Julian (2011) 'The Price of Mexico's "Drugs War"', BBC News, 19 April.

Millar, Bruce (2004) 'A Positive Drug Test?', *Sunday Times*, 23 May.

Misra, Amalenda (2004) *Afghanistan* (Polity).

Moran, Alice (2011) 'The Drugs (Policies) Don't Work', http://today.yougov. co.uk/life/drugs-policies-dont-work.

Moskos, Peter and Franklin, Neill (2009) 'Time to Legalize Drugs', *Washington Post*, 18 August.

Mott, Joy (1991) 'Crime and Heroin Use', in Philip Bean and David Whynes (eds), *Policing and Prescribing* (Macmillan).

Murji, Karim (1999) 'White Lines: Culture, "Race" and Drugs', in Nigel South (ed.), *Drugs, Cultures, Controls and Everyday Life* (Sage).

Musto, David (1999) *The American Disease*, (Oxford University Press).

Nadelman, E (1989) 'Drug Prohibition in the US: Costs, Consequences and Alternatives', *Science*, 245, 939–47.

Nair, Sunil (2003) 'Truth Hurts', *Guardian*, 29 January.

National Drug Control Budget FY2011 Funding Highlights (2010) https:// www.hsdl.org/?view&did=27354.

NDS News (2010) 28 April NDS @coi.95i.gov.uk.

Nemtsova, Anna (2010) 'Russian War on Drugs: Tackling the Heroin Problem Means Going Back to Afghanistan', *Telegraph*, 5 April.

Norman, Matthew (2009) 'Smokers Should Be Praised Not Blamed', *Independent*, 17 September.

Nutt, David (2009) 'My Views on Drugs Classification', *Guardian*, 3 November.

Observer editorial (2009) 'Drugs: Prejudice and Political Weakness Have Rejected Scientific Facts', 1 November.

Observer editorial (2010) 'A Unique Chance to Rethink Drug Policy', 8 August.

Office of National Statistics (ONS) (2008) 'Deaths Related to Drug Poisoning in England and Wales', www.statsitics.gov.uk.

Office of National Statistics (ONS) (2010) www.statistics.gov.uk, 24 August.

O'Grady, Mary Anastasia (2010) 'The War on Drugs is Doomed', *Wall Street Journal*, 22 March.

O'Neill, Ann (2008) 'Stakes Rise as Drug War Threatens to Cross the Border', CNN, 18 May.

Oxford Economic Outlook (2010) *Oxford Economic Outlook for the UK Drinks Sector Report 2010*. www.oef.com.

Page, Jeremy (2009) 'The Afghanistan Opium Crop: Buy It or Legalise It', *The Times*, 20 February.

Parker, Howard and Kirby, Perpetua (1996) 'Methadone Maintenance and Crime Reduction on Merseyside', Crime, Detection and Prevention Series Paper 72 (Home Office).

Parliamentary Research Branch (2009) Library of Parliament for the Senate Special Committee on Illegal Drugs: Dutch Drug Policy and Laws.

Peterkin, Tom (2009) 'SNP Curb on Drink Prices is Condemned in America', *Scotsman*, 12 September.

Phillips, Melanie (2008) 'Blame the Rich for Feeding the Drug Industry', *The Times*, 1 August.

Pillay, Navi (2009) cit Briefing 'The 10 Year Review of the UN Drug Control System' (IDPC).

Ramesh, Randeep (2010) 'Substance Abuse, Not Mental Illness Causes Violent Crime', *Guardian*, 6 September.

RAND (1994) 'Controlling Cocaine: Supply Versus Demand Programs' (RAND Corporation).

Reagan, Ronald (1986) Speech from Oval Office about Drugs, 12 September.

Reid, Melanie (2008) 'Blame the Rich for Feeding the Drug Industry', *The Times*, 1 August.

Reid Melanie (2009a) 'High Society: Everyone's Doing It', *The Times*, 19 October.

Reid, Melanie (2009b) 'Two Sozzled Victims of Modern Hypocrisy', *The Times*, 5 November.

Reid, Melanie (2010) 'No Law Will Stop People Wanting to Get High', *The Times* 1 April.

Release (2011) 'Drugs – It's Time for Better Laws – Letter to the Prime Minister', 2 June.

Reporter (no by-line) *Daily Mail* (2009) 'Taking Ecstasy No More Dangerous Than Horse Riding Says Government's Top Drug Adviser', 7 February.

Reuter Peter (2008) 'Can Production and Trafficking of Illicit Drugs be Reduced or Merely Shifted?', World Bank Political Research Working Paper 4564.

Reuter, Peter (2009a) 'The Unintended Consequences of Drug Policies', Report 5 (RAND Europe).

Reuter, Peter (2009b) 'Ten Years of UNGASS', *Addiction*, 104.

Robson, Philip (2005) 'Cannabis and Psychosis', BBC *Panorama*, 19 June.

Robson, Philip (2009) *Forbidden Drugs*, 3rd edn (Oxford University Press).

Rogers, Paul (2000) 'Britain's Secret War on Drugs', BBC *Panorama*, 2 October.

Rojas, Isaias (2005) 'Drug Policies, Human Rights and Democracy', in Coletta Youngers and Eileen Rosin (eds), *Drugs and Democracy in Latin America* (Lynne Reinner).

Rolles, Steve (2010) 'An Alternative to the War on Drugs', *British Medical Journal*, 13 July.

Rolleston Committee (1926) Report of the Departmental Committee on Morphine and Heroin (HMSO).

Romero, Simon (2010) 'Coca Production Makes a Comeback in Peru', *New York Times*, 13 June.

Rose, Gareth (2010) 'Drug Dealer Aged Ten is Arrested', *Scotsman*, 6 September.

Rosenberg, L.R. (1996) *American Drug War Debacle* (Avebury).

Royal College of Psychiatrists and Royal College of Physicians Working Party (2000) *Drugs, Dilemmas and Choices* (Gaskell).

Royal Commission on Opium 1894–5 British Parliamentary Papers.

Ruggiero, Vincenzo (1999) 'Drugs as a Password and the Law as a Drug: Discussing the Legalisation of Illicit Substances', in Nigel South (ed.), *Drugs, Cultures, Controls and Everyday Life* (Sage).

Ruggiero, V. and South, N. (1997) 'The Late Modern City as a Bazaar: Drug Markets, Illegal Enterprises and Their "Barricades"', *British Journal of Sociology* 48(1), 55–71.

Runciman, R (2000) 'Drugs and the Law: Report of the Independent Inquiry into the Misuse of Drugs Act 1971' (Police Foundation).

Sandmeyer, E.C. (1939) *The Anti-Chinese Movement in California* (The University of Illinois Press).

Sanderson, David and Fishburn, Alice (2010) 'Methadone for Jailed Heroin Addicts; Safety Net of Life Sentence', *The Times*, 17 March.

Santos, Francisco (2008) 'Shared Responsibility: Colombia's Proposal Against Drugs', Statement UN Center Japan 7 November.

Sare, Jeremy (2011) 'How the Media Helped to Ban Methedrone', *British Medical Journal*, 24 February.

Seddon, Toby (2010) *A History of Drugs* (Routledge).

Select Committee on Home Affairs Report (2002) 'The Government's Drug Policy: Is It Working?' (Home Office).

Senior, Antonia (2009) 'Drugs Are Evil, We Should Legalize Them Now', *The Times*, 31 July.

Shapiro, Harry (1999) 'Dances with Drugs: Pop Music, Drugs and Youth Culture', in Nigel South (ed.), *Drugs, Cultures, Controls and Everyday Life* (Sage).

Shapiro, Harry (2005) Interview with Tony Blair, *Druglink*, March/April.

Shapiro, Harry (2010) *Druglink*, March.

Shewan, David and Delgarno, Phil (2005) 'Evidence for Controlled Heroin Use? Low Levels of Negative Health and Social Outcomes Among Non-treatment Heroin Users in Glasgow', *British Journal of Health Psychology*, 10, 33–48.

Simpson, Mark (2003) 'Relationship Between Drug Use and Crime: A Puzzle Inside an Enigma', *International Journal of Drug Policy*, 14(4), 307–19.

Sirotu, David (2010) 'We're Paying Too High a Price for the War on Drugs', *Seattle Times*, 11 April.

Skinner, Quentin (1978) *Foundations of Modern Political Thought*, vol. 1 (Cambridge University Press).

Slack, James (2009) 'Drugs Tsar Sacked for Claiming Ecstasy, Cannabis and LSD are Less Harmful Than Alcohols Says More Advisors Will Quit', *Daily Mail*, 31 October.

Stares, Paul (1996) *Global Habit* (Brookings Institute).

Steele, John (2007) '70 Addicts Kick Drugs at a Cost of £1.85 Million Each', *Telegraph*, 31 October.

Stem, V. (1998) *A Sin Against the Future: Imprisonment in the World* (Penguin).

Stevens, Alex (2010) 'Britain's Drug Policy Will Not Improve Until We Are Bold Enough to Experiment', *Observer*, 5 September.

Stimson, Gerry and Metrebin, Nicky (2003) *Prescribing Heroin: What is the Evidence?* (Joseph Rowntree Foundation).

Stoker, Peter (2004) 'Pupils in US Welcome Drug Tests', BBC News, 22 February.

Streatfeild, Dominic (2001) *Cocaine – An Unauthorised Biography* (Virgin).

Suddath, Claire (2009) 'The War on Drugs', *Time*, 25 March.

'The Economics of Tobacco', Business – The Company File (1999), BBC, 29 September.

'The Right Sentence' (2009) *Washington Post*, 29 October.

Thoumi, Francisco E. (1992) 'Why the Illegal Psychoactive Drugs Industry Grew in Colombia', *Journal of Interamerican Studies and World Affairs*, 34(3), 37–63.

Thoumi, Francisco and Navarrette-Frias, Carolina (2009) 'Illegal Drugs and Human Rights of Peasants and Indigenous Communities: The Case of Peru', Management of Social Transformation Policy Paper 13.

Time (2010) 'Mexico Narco-Insurgency', 3 March.

Tobacco Economics www.the-tma.org.uk/tobacco-tax-revenue,aspx.

Tobacco Working for America http://fujipub.com/fot/working.html.

Townsend, Mark (2010) 'Police Chief Issues Call to Decriminalize Cannabis and Redirect Resources', *Guardian*, 18 September.

Townsend, Mark (2010) 'Why Britain Tops the World Drug Use League', *Observer* 14 November.

Transnational Institute (1999) 'Drug Wars in the Skies' (TNI).

Travis, Alan (2002) 'Crack Warning for the Young – Move to Stop Pupils Choosing Dealing as a Career', *Guardian*, 24 December.

Travis, Alan (2009) 'Alcohol Worse Than Ecstasy – Drugs Chief', *Guardian*, 29 October.

Travis, Alan (2011) 'Decriminalize Possession of Drugs Celebrities Urge Government', *Guardian*, 2 June.

Trebach, Arnold S. and Inciardi, James A. (1993) *Legalize It?* (American University Press).

United Kingdom Drug Policy Consortium (UKDPC) (2009) 'Police Cannot Win Drugs War and Should Focus on Damage Limitation', Press Briefing, 30 July.

United Kingdom Drug Situation Report 2009 (Home Office).

UNAIDS (2010) 'Call for Urgent Action to Improve Coverage of HIV Services for Injecting Drug Users', 10 March.

UNDCP (1995) 'The Social Impact of Drugs' for the World Summit for Social Development 47. Available online at http://www.unodc.org/pdf/technical_series_1995-03-01_1.pdf.

UNODC (2009a) Report: Drug Use in Afghanistan.

UNODC Reports Rise in Opium (2009b) www.voanews.com/english/news/asia/UN-Reports-Rise-in-Opium-Cultivation-in-Burma-79218497.html.

UNODC (2010) Interview with Colombian Vice President, http://www.unodc.org/unodc/en/frontpage/interview-with-the-colombian-vice-preseident.html.

Vancouver Sun (2011) 'Extra-strength Heroin Claims 20 Lives in Lower Mainland: Coroner', 9 May.

Vass, Beck (2010) 'Supermarkets are Drug Pushers, Says Lobbyist', *New Zealand Herald*, 30 August.

Walsh, John M (2008) 'US Drug Policy: At What Cost?' Presentation to US Congress.

Wakerfield, Bruno (2010) 'Dutch to Ban Drug Tourists', *Telegraph*, 24 August.

Weaver, Matthew (2010) 'CIA Footage Broadcast of Fatal Attack on Plane Carrying US Missionaries in Peru', *Guardian*, 4 February.

Weil, Andrew MD (1986) *The Natural Mind: An Investigation of Drugs and Higher Consciousness* (Houghton Mifflin).

Werb, D., Mills, Edward J., Debeck, Kora, Kerr, Thomas, Montaner, Julio S.G. and Wood, Evan (2010a) 'The Effectiveness of Anti-Illicit-Drug Public-Service Announcements: A Systematic Review and Meta-Analysis', *Epidemiol Community Health.*

Werb, D., Rowell, G., Gayatt, G et al. (2010b) 'The Effect of Drug Law Enforcement on Drug Related Violence' (Vancouver International Centre for Science in Drug Policy).

Wilbert, J. (1987) *Tobacco and Shamanism in South America* (Yale University Press).

Wilson, James Q. (1990) 'Against the Legalization of Drugs', in Ross Coomber (ed.), *Drug and Drug Use in Society* (Greenwich University Press).

Wisotsky, Steven (1990) 'International Law Enforcement: The Futile Quest for Control of Coca and Cocaine at Sources', in Coomber, Ross (ed.), *Drug and Drug Use in Society* (Greenwich University Press).

Women's Petition against Coffee (1674) Available online at www.gopetition.com.

Whynes, David (1991) 'Illicit Drug Production and Supply-Side Drugs Policy in Asia and South America', *Development and Change* 22 (Sage).

WHO/UNICRI (1995) *Cocaine Project Report* (WHO/UNICRI).

World Drug Report 2010. www.unodc.org/unodc/en/data-and.../WDR-2010.html.

Yang-wen, Zheng (2001) *The Social Life of Opium in China* (Cambridge University Press).

YouGov (2011) 'The Drugs (Policies) Don't Work'. Available online at http://today.yougov.co.uk/life/drugs-policies-dont-work.

Youngers, Coletta A. (2011) 'The Obama Administration's Drug Control Policy on Auto-pilot', IDPC Briefing Paper, April (IDPC).

Index